U.S. Global Health Assistance: FY2014-FY2016 Appropriations

Background

The President's FY2016 budget request included more than $9 billion for global health assistance, including roughly $8 billion through State, Foreign Operations appropriation and (SFOPs) some $910 million through Department of Labor, Health and Human Services (Labor-HHS), and Education appropriation. In FY2016 omnibus appropriations, Congress provided more than the Administration sought for global health programs through SFOPs but less than requested for Labor-HHS.

State Foreign Operations Appropriations

Congress funds the President's Emergency Plan for AIDS Relief (PEPFAR), the Global Fund to Fight AIDS, Tuberculosis and Malaria (Global Fund), and global health activities implemented by the U.S. Agency for International Development (USAID) through State, Foreign Operations appropriations (SFOPs). In SFOPs, global health funding remained level from FY2015 to FY2016, except for malaria, maternal and child health (MCH), and nutrition programs, which all received funding increases.

Figure 1. Foreign Operations Appropriations: FY2014-FY2016

(current U.S. $ millions and percent)

Agency/Program	FY2014 Enacted	FY2015 Enacted	FY2016 Request	FY2016 Enacted
State HIV/AIDS	4,020	4,320	4,319	4,320
State Global Fund	1,569	1,350	1,107	1,350
STATE-GHP TOTAL	5,670	5,670	5,426	5,670
USAID HIV/AIDS	330	330	330	330
Tuberculosis	236	236	191	236
Malaria	665	670	674	674
Maternal and Child Health	705	715	770	750
Nutrition	115	115	101	125
Vulnerable Children	22	22	15	22
FP/RH	524	524	538	524
NTDs	100	100	87	100
Global Health Security	73	73	50	73
USAID-GHP TOTAL	2,770	2,784	2,755	2,834
FOREIGN OPS TOTAL	8,440	8,454	8,181	8,504

Source: Created by CRS from FY2016 State, Foreign Operations Congressional Budget Justification and explanatory notes of the FY2015 Consolidated Appropriations.

Notes: Excludes emergency appropriations for Ebola and global health funds provided through other USAID accounts, such as the International Disaster Assistance (IDA) account.

USAID groups its global health programs into three key areas: saving mothers and children, creating an AIDS-Free generation, and fighting other infectious diseases.

Significant progress has been made in each of these areas, though challenges remain.

Maternal and Child Health

International efforts to improve health care during pregnancy and childbirth has resulted in a 45% reduction in maternal deaths from 523,000 in 1990 to 289,000 maternal deaths in 2013. Roughly one-third of these deaths occurred in Nigeria and India. Human resource constraints continue to complicate efforts to reduce maternal mortality. In many developing countries, especially in sub-Saharan Africa, pregnant women often deliver their babies without the assistance of trained health practitioners who can help to avert deaths caused by hemorrhage. The World Health Organization (WHO) estimates that 27% of all maternal deaths are caused by severe bleeding. Preexisting conditions like HIV/AIDS and malaria are also key contributors to maternal mortality, accounting for roughly 28% of maternal deaths.

International efforts to improve child health have roughly cut the number of child deaths in half from 12.7 million in 1990 to almost 6 million in 2015. WHO estimates that more than half of the 16,000 child deaths that occurred in each day of 2013 could have been avoided through low-cost interventions, such as medicines to treat pneumonia, diarrhea, and malaria, as well as tools that prevent the transmission of malaria and HIV/AIDS from mother to child. Other factors, like inadequate access to nutritious food, also affect child health. WHO estimates that undernutrition contributes to roughly 45% of all child deaths. The risk of a child dying is at its highest within the first month of life, when 44% of all child deaths occur. Children in sub-Saharan Africa are more than 15 times more likely to die before reaching age five than their counterparts in developed countries.

USAID requested an 8% increase in funding for maternal and child health programs. FY2016 appropriations for USAID maternal and child health programs were higher than the FY2015 level, but less than the Administration's request.

HIV/AIDS

In 2013, roughly 2.1 million people worldwide contracted HIV, roughly 40% less than new infections in 2000. More than 70% of new HIV cases occurred in sub-Saharan Africa. While the number of new cases is declining, the number of people living with HIV is rising. In 2013, more than 35 million people were living with HIV globally. Expanded access to anti-retroviral treatments (ART) has decreased the number of people dying from AIDS-related causes. In 2012, 1.5 million people died from HIV/AIDS, down from the peak of 2.3 million in 2005 (**Figure 2**).

Figure 2. AIDS Deaths Worldwide: 1995-2014

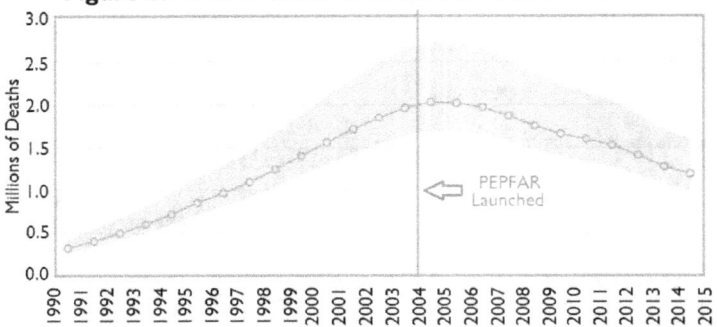

Source: Adapted by CRS from the Joint United Nations Program on AIDS (UNAIDS) webpage, *AIDSinfo*, http://aidsinfo.unaids.org/, accessed on December 18, 2015.

The United States has contributed substantially to improving global access to ART through PEPFAR and its support for the Global Fund to Fight AIDS, Tuberculosis and Malaria. By June 2014, 12.1 million people in low- and middle-income countries were receiving ART. At the end of FY2015, PEPFAR was supporting the provision of ART to more than 9.5 million people, thereby supporting treatment for more than half of all HIV-positive people in low- and middle-income countries. For FY2016, the Administration requested no change for PEPFAR funding, but proposed a reduction in support to the Global Fund. Congress maintained funding at FY2015 levels for PEFPAR and the Global Fund.

Other Infectious Diseases

In recent years, a succession of new and reemerging infectious diseases have caused outbreaks and pandemics that have affected thousands of people worldwide: Severe Acute Respiratory Syndrome (SARS, 2003), Avian Influenza H5N1 (2005), Pandemic Influenza H1N1 (2009), Middle East Respiratory Syndrome coronavirus (MERS-CoV, 2013), and the ongoing Ebola outbreak in West Africa. The incapacity of Guinea, Liberia, and Sierra Leone to contain and end the ongoing Ebola epidemic has revealed the threat that weak health systems pose to the world. The United States plays a leading role in the Global Health Security Agenda, a multilateral effort to improve the capacity of countries worldwide to detect, prevent, and respond to diseases with pandemic potential.

At the same time that the world faces threats from new diseases, long-standing diseases like tuberculosis (TB) continue to pose a threat to global health security. Among infectious diseases, TB is the second most common cause of death worldwide. Multi-drug resistant (MDR)-TB is of growing concern, as it is more expensive and difficult to treat. Less than half of all MDR-TB patients survive. WHO asserts that global funding for addressing MDR-TB is insufficient and weaknesses in health systems complicate efforts to treat the disease and prevent its further spread. Despite the threat that infectious diseases pose to the world, the FY2016 budget proposed reducing funding for all USAID infectious disease programs, except malaria. Enacted FY2016 appropriations for infectious diseases programs remained level, except for malaria, which received a $4 million increase.

Labor, HHS Appropriations

The FY2016 budget request included an 8% increase for global health programs implemented by the Centers for Disease Control and Prevention (CDC) and a 2% boost for international HIV/AIDS research conducted by the National Institutes of Health (NIH, **Figure 3**). Budgetary increases were aimed at two key priorities for CDC: eradicating polio and accelerating efforts to improve pandemic preparedness.

Figure 3. Labor-HHS Appropriations: FY2014-FY2016
(current U.S. $ millions)

Agency/Program	FY2014 Enacted	FY2015 Enacted	FY2016 Request	FY2016 Enacted
HIV/AIDS	128.7	128.4	128.4	128.4
Immunizations	200.9	208.6	218.6	219.0
Polio	150.9	158.8	168.8	169.0
Measles	50.0	49.8	49.8	50.0
Parasitic Disease/Malaria	24.4	24.4	24.4	24.5
Global Public Health Protection	62.8	55.1	76.7	55.2
CDC TOTAL	416.8	416.5	448.1	427.1
NIH Global AIDS Research	453.6	451.2	462.2	462.2
LABOR-HHS TOTAL	**870.4**	**867.7**	**910.3**	**889.3**

Source: Created by CRS from FY2016 State, Foreign Operations Congressional Budget Justification.

Notes: Excludes appropriations for Ebola. Congress does not specify the amount the Office of AIDS Research should spend on global AIDS research. The FY2016 amount equals the budget request.

Eradicating Polio

Expanded access to vaccines has contributed significantly to global declines in child deaths. According to the CDC, 80% of the world is now polio-free and polio cases have declined by more than 99% from 1998 levels. The disease is endemic in only three countries: Afghanistan, Nigeria, and Pakistan. Polio activities are part of broader efforts to expand access to vaccine-preventable illnesses, such as measles. Global vaccine efforts have reduced measles deaths by 75% from 2000 levels.

Pandemic Preparedness and Global Health Security

In the FY2016 budget request, CDC reported that it responded to 268 global disease outbreaks in 2013, provided assistance to over 145 humanitarian missions in 35 countries, and projected that it would respond globally to at least 100 disease outbreaks in 2016. CDC requested an additional $22 million to deepen U.S. engagement in the Global Health Security Agenda. Congress did not fund the budget increase, but provided CDC $597 million through FY2015 Emergency Ebola appropriations for global pandemic preparedness. For information on emergency Ebola appropriations, see CRS Report R43807, *FY2015 Funding to Counter Ebola and the Islamic State (IS)*.

Tiaji Salaam-Blyther, tsalaam@crs.loc.gov, 7-7677

IF10131

Zika Virus: CRS Experts

Sarah A. Lister
Specialist in Public Health and Epidemiology

February 17, 2016

Congressional Research Service
7-5700
www.crs.gov
R44385

The following table provides names and contact information for CRS experts on policy concerns relating to the global spread of the Zika virus. Policy areas include the following:

- health system preparedness and response (domestic and global);
- countries in Latin America and the Caribbean;
- mosquito control;
- medical product development and regulation;
- women's health;
- U.S. emergency management;
- legal issues; and
- miscellaneous.

The following acronyms are used:

- BARDA: Biomedical Advanced Research and Development Authority
- EPA: Environmental Protection Agency
- FDA: Food and Drug Administration
- FEMA: Federal Emergency Management Agency
- FIFRA: Federal Insecticide, Fungicide, and Rodenticide Act
- NIH: National Institutes of Health
- USOC: U.S. Olympic Committee.

Legislative Issues	Name/Title	Phone	Email
Health System Preparedness and Response			
Domestic activities	**Sarah A. Lister** Specialist in Public Health and Epidemiology	7-7320	slister@crs.loc.gov
	C. Stephen Redhead Specialist in Health Policy	7-2261	credhead@crs.loc.gov
Global activities	**Tiaji Salaam-Blyther** Specialist in Global Health	7-7677	tsalaam@crs.loc.gov
Latin America and the Caribbean			
	June S. Beittel Analyst in Latin American Affairs	7-7613	jbeittel@crs.loc.gov
	Peter J. Meyer Analyst in Latin American Affairs	7-5474	pmeyer@crs.loc.gov
	Clare Ribando Seelke Specialist in Latin American Affairs	7-5229	cseelke@crs.loc.gov
	Mark P. Sullivan Specialist in Latin American Affairs	7-7689	msullivan@crs.loc.gov
	Maureen Taft-Morales Specialist in Latin American Affairs	7-7659	mtmorales@crs.loc.gov

Legislative Issues	Name/Title	Phone	Email
Mosquito Control			
Ecology and entomology	**M. Lynne Corn** Specialist in Natural Resources Policy	7-7267	lcorn@crs.loc.gov
EPA-regulated products: pesticides, including repellents	**Jerry H. Yen** Analyst in Environmental Policy:	7-9113	jyen@crs.loc.gov
	Robert Esworthy Specialist in Environmental Policy	7-7236	resworthy@crs.loc.gov
Genetically engineered mosquitoes	**Tadlock Cowan** Analyst in Natural Resources and Rural Development	7-7600	tcowan@crs.loc.gov
Public health recommendations, U.S. state control programs	**Sarah A. Lister** Specialist in Public Health and Epidemiology	7-7320	slister@crs.loc.gov
Medical Product Development and Regulation			
Basic biomedical research, NIH	**Judith A. Johnson** Specialist in Biomedical Policy	7-7077	jajohnson@crs.loc.gov
Product development: Project BioShield, BARDA	**Frank Gottron** Specialist in Science and Technology Policy	7-5854	fgottron@crs.loc.gov
FDA regulation of drugs	**Agata Dabrowska** Analyst in Health Policy	7-9455	adabrowska@crs.loc.gov
FDA regulation of vaccines and diagnostic tests	**Judith A. Johnson** Specialist in Biomedical Policy	7-7077	jajohnson@crs.loc.gov
Women's Health			
Women's reproductive health; domestic	**Judith A. Johnson** Specialist in Biomedical Policy	7-7077	jajohnson@crs.loc.gov
U.S. international family planning policy; global	**Luisa Blanchfield** Specialist in International Relations	7-0856	lblanchfield@crs.loc.gov
U.S. Emergency Management			
Stafford Act, FEMA disaster declarations	**Francis X. McCarthy** Analyst in Emergency Management Policy	7-9533	fmccarthy@crs.loc.gov
Stafford Act, FEMA grant assistance	**Jared T. Brown** Analyst in Emergency Management and Homeland Security Policy	7-4918	jbrown@crs.loc.gov
Legal Issues			
U.S. public health	**Jared P. Cole** Legislative Attorney	7-6350	jpcole@crs.loc.gov
FDA	**Jennifer A. Staman** Legislative Attorney	7-2610	jstaman@crs.loc.gov
Abortion, family planning	**Jon O. Shimabukuro** Legislative Attorney	7-7990	jshimabukuro@crs.loc.gov
FIFRA, regulation of pesticides	**Alexandra M. Wyatt** Legislative Attorney	7-0816	awyatt@crs.loc.gov
Miscellaneous			
2016 Summer Olympic Games in Rio de Janeiro: USOC and U.S. issues	**L. Elaine Halchin** Specialist in American National Government	7-0646	ehalchin@crs.loc.gov

Legislative Issues	Name/Title	Phone	Email
2016 Summer Olympic Games in Rio de Janeiro: issues re: Brazil	**Peter J. Meyer** Analyst in Latin American Affairs	7-5474	pmeyer@crs.loc.gov
Environmental review of federal actions	**Linda Luther** Analyst in Environmental Policy	7-6852	lluther@crs.loc.gov

Author Contact Information

Sarah A. Lister
Specialist in Public Health and Epidemiology
slister@crs.loc.gov, 7-7320

Mosquitoes, Zika Virus, and Transmission Ecology

The Zika virus is transmitted primarily by mosquitoes, and the Centers for Disease Control and Prevention (CDC) have identified some cases of human-to-human transmittal. The two species of mosquitoes most commonly associated with transmitting the virus are the yellow fever mosquito (*Aedes aegypti*, or YFM) and Asian tiger mosquito (*Aedes albopictus*, or ATM). This report will focus on the ecology of the two mosquito species and briefly discuss methods used or proposed either to control their populations or to limit their ability to transmit viruses. Control methods could require compliance with a variety of federal or state statutes and regulations; such statutes generally have special provisions regarding human health and safety. For a discussion of human health issues, see CRS Report R44368, *Zika Virus: Basics About the Disease*, and CRS Insight IN10433, *Zika Virus: Global Health Considerations*.

Mosquito Ecology

Neither mosquito is native to the Western Hemisphere. YFM is native to Africa, and ATM is from Southeast Asia. Only females bite; blood proteins are then used in egg development. After a blood meal from an infected person, a virus may be transmitted to a person bitten later. Both mosquitoes are vectors for other human viruses, including dengue fever, chikungunya, and yellow fever. As a result of their association with these major and established diseases, considerable research on their ecology has been performed. Both species are strongly associated with human habitat, particularly YFM, which is a weaker flyer and rarely travels more than a few hundred yards in its lifetime. However, both are hitchhikers and may spread via cars, planes, and boats.

Both species are already found in suitable habitat along the U.S. Gulf Coast, and both occur sporadically in parts of California, Arizona, and New Mexico. However, ATM has adapted to cooler temperatures, allowing it to spread into higher elevations and farther north. Its range currently extends north into Pennsylvania and west to parts of Iowa and Nebraska.

Both species breed in small containers of fresh water. Breeding sites may include roadside rubbish, discarded tires, flower pots, gutters, potholes, and even bottle caps. The larvae of both are aquatic, and at the larval stage their predators include other insects. When they emerge from the larval stage, predators include dragonflies, birds, and bats. Both species are primarily diurnal (i.e., active in daytime). Both avoid biting humans who have recently used various registered repellants.

Controlling Mosquito Numbers

Control methods for the two species are varied and include elimination of breeding sites and pesticide applications, as well as screening and well-sealed homes. Issues include efficacy, cost, and human or environmental health.

Figure 1. Approximate U.S. Distribution of Zika Virus Vectors

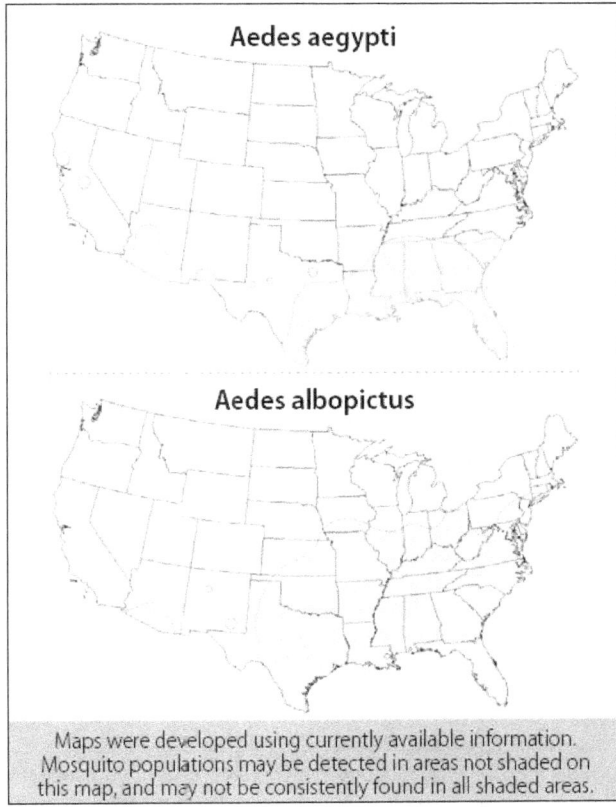

Maps were developed using currently available information. Mosquito populations may be detected in areas not shaded on this map, and may not be consistently found in all shaded areas.

Source: National Center for Emerging and Zoonotic Infectious Diseases, Centers for Disease Control and Prevention.

Reducing the Sources: Breeding Sites

Reduction of breeding sites as a mosquito-control method was most famously tested in 1904, not long after the discovery of the link between mosquitoes and disease transmission, with the building of the Panama Canal. It continues to be used, especially in the South. The method is still effective but requires broad public participation and education for success. Public funding for cleanup of roadside litter, destruction of old tires, and similar measures may be required.

Mosquitoes and Registered Pesticides

If habitat elimination or modification and other abatement approaches are not feasible or successful, requisite control strategies may require communities to rely on pesticides, particularly those used at the aquatic, larval stage. The U.S. Environmental Protection Agency (EPA) has registered a number of pesticides under the Federal Insecticide,

Fungicide, and Rodenticide Act (FIFRA) specifically for the domestic control of mosquitoes. (Some additional unregistered pesticides manufactured in the United States may be exported and used abroad but not domestically.) CDC guidelines recommend that decisions to use pesticides to control mosquitoes should be based on surveillance data and the risk of human disease. Registered pesticides include those to control mosquitoes at the larval stage (larvicides) in the breeding habitat before they can mature, ranging from bacterial insecticides, growth inhibitors, and organophosphate insecticides, to mineral oils and monomolecular films. There are also registered pesticides for controlling adult mosquitoes (adulticides), including synthetic pyrethroid insecticides and organophosphate insecticides. A more detailed list and discussion of registered pesticides are available from the National Pesticide Information Center (http://npic.orst.edu/pest/mosquito/mosqcides html) and from the EPA (http://www.epa.gov/mosquitocontrol).

Further, an exemption process exists for circumstances in which no efficacious pesticide is currently registered. Under Section 18 of FIFRA (7 U.S.C. 136p; regulations in 40 C.F.R., Part 166), state or federal agencies may request an Emergency Public Health exemption to use a non-registered pesticide when they deem that a pest will cause a significant risk to human health. Emergency Public Health exemptions must be approved by EPA and may be authorized for up to one year. An Emergency Public Health exemption was granted for the control for ticks carrying Lyme disease, for example.

Preventing Transmission of the Virus

Alternatives to attempting to kill substantial numbers of mosquitoes directly include attempting to reduce the ability of the mosquitoes to transmit viruses or to reduce the number of viable offspring. Neither method has been fully tested in the field with respect to Zika virus.

Release of Genetically Modified Mosquitoes

Genetic engineering has been used to create mosquitoes that either are not able to carry the disease-causing pathogens or are unable to produce viable offspring. For example, researchers are genetically engineering mosquitoes to make them more resistant to the *Plasmodium* parasite that causes malaria. Other researchers are developing mosquitoes to express antimalarial peptides and enzymes that inhibit parasite development. These varieties have not been field tested and hence are not approved.

In 2002, scientists at the British firm Oxitec genetically modified some YFM so that larvae die unless they are exposed to the antibiotic tetracycline. When males are released into the wild, where tetracycline is generally absent, males mate with wild females to produce larvae that die before they reach adulthood. These genetically modified mosquitoes were field tested by the company in 2009-2011 in Grand Cayman Islands, Malaysia, and Brazil. Oxitec reported that YFM populations were significantly reduced within the test areas. Similar plans to field test these engineered mosquitoes in the Florida Keys in 2012 were halted after environmental, regulatory, and ethical issues were raised. The U.S. Food and Drug Administration's

Center for Veterinary Medicine is currently reviewing the potential environmental and human health effects of a U.S field test of the mosquitoes under its Investigational New Animal Drug protocol.

Mosquito Bacteria to Suppress Virus

Another approach focuses primarily on reducing mosquitoes' ability to transmit viruses. Researchers in Australia infected YFM with a bacterium called *Wolbachia*, which naturally infects many other insect species, though not YFM. The bacterium appears to limit the multiplication of the dengue virus inside the mosquito, thus limiting the chance of transmitting dengue to the next victim. The bacterium is too big to pass through a mosquito's mouthparts into a human, but infected females pass it via their eggs into their offspring.

When *Wolbachia*-infected males mate with uninfected females, their offspring fail to hatch. But because infected females pass the bacterium on to their offspring, the bacterium eventually spreads through the entire population, both in the laboratory and in certain field trials. Field trials in Australia appeared to be successful in ending chronic dengue fever outbreaks. Further trials are continuing in Southeast Asia, and one trial began in Brazil in 2015. Because the dengue, chikungunya, and Zika viruses are similar (all RNA viruses), *Wolbachia* has been suggested as a potentially useful tool against Zika as well.

Conclusion

No single method of controlling YFM or ATM seems likely to be effective in completely eliminating transmission of Zika virus, nor in extirpating either mosquito species from the Western Hemisphere. Surveillance for the presence of YFM and ATM and public cooperation in reducing breeding sites are prerequisites for local policy choices. Multiple tools are available or being tested; in conjunction they may lessen or break transmission of the Zika virus through mosquitoes.

M. Lynne Corn, lcorn@crs.loc.gov, 7-7267
Tadlock Cowan, tcowan@crs.loc.gov, 7-7600
Robert Esworthy, resworthy@crs.loc.gov, 7-7236

IF10353

Dominican Republic

The Dominican Republic occupies the eastern two-thirds of the Caribbean island of Hispaniola, which it shares with Haiti. The Dominican Republic is one of the most important countries in the Caribbean for U.S. policy because of its large size, strong economy, and stability. The United States is the Dominican Republic's main trading partner; two-way trade totaled more than $11.8 billion in 2015. The U.S. government is supporting efforts to improve education, resilience to climate change, services for those with HIV/AIDS, citizen security, and protections for vulnerable populations in the country. Recently, U.S. interest has focused on the citizenship status and treatment of Dominicans of Haitian descent and undocumented people.

Dominican-Haitian relations have historically been strained. Haiti is the Dominican Republic's second-largest trade partner, and the Dominican government provided significant support to help Haiti rebuild after the 2010 earthquake. Nevertheless, continued instability in Haiti is of great concern to the Dominican government. Disputes over migration and trade led to Haiti banning Dominican imports worth some $500 million in late 2015.

Background

After fighting to achieve its independence from Spain in 1821 and then from Haiti in 1844, the Dominican Republic embarked upon a bumpy road toward democracy that included coups, dictatorships, and U.S. interventions (including 1916-1924 and 1965-1966). Rafael Trujillo ruled the country as dictator from 1930 to 1961, employing violent tactics to quell opposition. Despite his brutality, Trujillo's anticommunist stance earned him tacit U.S. support. His acolyte, Joaquín Balaguer, served as president from 1960 to 1962, 1966 to 1978, and 1986 to 1996. As a result of the dominance of these *caudillo* (strongman) leaders, the Dominican Republic did not develop into a modern democracy until the 1990s. In 1994, an agreement commonly referred to as the Pact for Democracy removed Balaguer from power and paved the way for the country's first free and fair elections in 1996.

Since that time, the Dominican Republic, for the most part, has seen solid economic growth and developed democratic institutions, albeit with high levels of corruption. Led by former president Leonel Fernández (1996-2000, 2004-2012) and current President Danilo Medina, the center-left Dominican Liberation Party (PLD) has solidified its dominance over Dominican politics. Medina boosted tax revenues upon taking office in 2012 and has since devoted significant resources to education, health care, and support to small businesses, with positive outcomes in those areas. Many observers have praised the PLD's economic stewardship but expressed concerns that one-party rule may have eroded pluralism in the country. The main opposition

party, the Dominican Revolutionary Party (PRD), ran in an alliance with the PLD in the 2016 elections.

Figure 1. Dominican Republic Facts

Capital: Santo Domingo

Population: 10.5 million

Comparative Area: size of Vermont and New Hampshire combined

Ethnic Groups: 73% mixed, 16% European, 11% African origin

Literacy: 91.8%

Life Expectancy: 78.0 years

GDP; GDP per capita: $64.1 billion; $6,040 per capita

Source: CRS graphic. Map data from Department of State, Figures from CIA World Factbook and World Bank, 2016.

Political Situation

On May 15, 2016, the Dominican Republic held federal (presidential and congressional) and municipal elections. As predicted, current President Medina, standing for a PLD-PRD alliance, defeated Luis Abinader of the Modern Revolutionary Party (formed by PRD dissidents) by a margin of 62% to 35% in elections that were generally regarded as free and fair. Medina is scheduled to be inaugurated to a second four-year term in August 2016.

President Medina likely will begin his second term in a favorable position. He will enjoy a legislative majority, as the PLD-PRD alliance captured a majority in the Dominican senate and chamber of deputies, albeit by a narrower margin than it had previously. The International Monetary Fund predicts that the Dominican economy will continue to expand in the coming years, although it will do so at a slower pace. The country is seeing the benefits of the government's prior investments in social programs, but several challenges remain to be addressed, including the following:

- **Naturalization and Regularization Plan.** According to criteria for acquiring Dominican nationality outlined in the 2010 constitution, children born in the Dominican Republic to parents in the country illegally are ineligible for citizenship. A September 2013 tribunal ruling applied that criterion retroactively to descendants of all undocumented migrants born in the country since 1929. Observers maintain that the ruling could render thousands of individuals stateless.

The Medina government developed a process to help resolve the citizenship status of those affected by the ruling. In May 2014, the Dominican Congress approved a *naturalization law* allowing some 55,000 individuals whose Dominican documents were invalidated by the ruling to keep their citizenship and register their children as citizens. It also provided a *naturalization plan* for individuals born in the country without documents who registered by February 1, 2015. Dominican officials maintain that they are willing to fix the citizenship status of anyone brought to their attention who missed that deadline. Many people lack the documents needed to prove their place of birth, in part because some Dominican officials have not historically issued identity documents to people perceived to be of Haitian descent.

In November 2013, the Dominican government launched a *regularization plan* that gave migrants born outside the country 18 months to register for legal non-immigrant status through a process that ended in June 2015. More than 288,400 people applied, of whom almost 240,000 qualified.

Deportations resumed in August 2015 after an 18-month hiatus while the regularization plan was implemented. The Dominican government maintains that its deportation policies are designed to prevent unjust expulsion or family separation. The Haitian government and human rights groups remain concerned that Dominicans of Haitian descent may be deported.

- **Drug Trafficking.** According to U.S. government estimates, the majority of the roughly 6% of U.S.- and Europe-bound cocaine that transits Hispaniola passes through the Dominican Republic using maritime routes. The Dominican Republic cooperates closely with the United States in counterdrug efforts through seizures, joint operations, and extraditions of drug-trafficking suspects. Cooperation has been hindered, however, by the complicity of corrupt police and other officials.

- **Corruption.** The Dominican Republic ranked 103rd out of 168 countries in Transparency International's 2015 Corruption Perceptions Index. The country's weak press and judicial systems have failed to investigate or punish cases of official corruption. PLD Senator Felix Bautista, who has been accused of diverting millions in public funds and bribing the former president of Haiti for contracts, has avoided prosecution even though his case was named one of the world's 15 worst examples of grand corruption in 2015 by Transparency International.

Economic Conditions

The Dominican Republic is among the fastest-growing economies in Latin America and the Caribbean (with 7% GDP growth in 2014 and 2015). It has the largest stock of foreign direct investment and the most diversified export structure of any country party to the Dominican Republic-Central America-United States Free Trade Agreement

(CAFTA-DR) except the United States. Remittances have exceeded $3.0 billion annually since 2010. High levels of foreign investment, solid mining and telecommunications sector performance, and strong tourism revenues have boosted growth. Tourism has not yet been affected by the Zika virus outbreak, although this could become an issue for the government.

Despite its impressive economic performance, low oil prices have masked the Dominican Republic's continued (though lessening) dependence on foreign oil for electricity generation and problems with its electricity sector. The government has made some effort to target subsidies to the poorest households and to criminalize nonpayment of bills. Nevertheless, the grid remains fragile, electricity losses are significant, and blackouts continue.

Poverty and inequality in the Dominican Republic are higher than the regional averages. According to a 2015 U.N. report, only 1 of the country's 32 provinces has a high level of human development. Despite government efforts, poverty stood at 37% in 2014.

U.S. Relations

The Dominican Republic enjoys a strong relationship with the United States, with extensive cultural, economic, and political ties. Vice President Biden highlighted the importance of those ties during a June 2014 visit to the country, the first by any U.S. vice president since 1980. No sitting U.S. president has visited the country. Currently, more than 1.5 million Dominicans reside in the United States. In recent decades, the United States has supported democracy, citizen security, and economic development in the Dominican Republic.

Congress oversees U.S. bilateral aid to the Dominican Republic, which has averaged roughly $22 million in recent years. Congress also provides funding and oversight of the Caribbean Basin Security Initiative (CBSI), a regional program through which the Dominican Republic has received law-enforcement training and equipment. Through CBSI, U.S. funds have helped to create a canine regional training facility and an anti-money laundering agency. U.S. humanitarian assistance provided through the International Organization for Migration and U.N. entities is helping to address citizenship and migration issues. U.S. assistance to bolster Zika response efforts is possible.

Congress also monitors CAFTA-DR and related issues, as well as how that and other free trade agreements may be affected by the proposed Trans-Pacific Partnership (TPP). Concerns have periodically emerged. The U.S. Department of Labor (DOL) has investigated complaints about forced and child labor in the Dominican sugarcane industry; DOL and the Dominican government are working to address these complaints. Dominican apparel producers are concerned that TPP would allow Vietnam and other Asian apparel producers to export clothing to the United States on more favorable terms than CAFTA-DR, reducing their competitive advantage.

Clare Ribando Seelke, cseelke@crs.loc.gov, 7-5229

IF10407

Pesticide Use and Water Quality: Are the Laws Complementary or in Conflict?

Claudia Copeland
Specialist in Resources and Environmental Policy

May 31, 2016

Congressional Research Service
7-5700
www.crs.gov
RL32884

Summary

This report provides background on the emerging conflict over interpretation and implementation of the Federal Insecticide, Fungicide, and Rodenticide Act (FIFRA) and the Clean Water Act (CWA). For the more than 30 years since they were enacted, there had been little apparent conflict between them. But their relationship has recently been challenged in several arenas, including the federal courts and regulatory proceedings of the Environmental Protection Agency (EPA). In this report, a brief discussion of the two laws is followed by a review of the major litigation of interest. EPA's efforts to clarify its policy in this area are discussed, including a regulation issued in 2006 that was subsequently vacated by a federal court, as well as possible options for EPA and Congress to address the issues further.

FIFRA governs the labeling, distribution, sale, and use of pesticides, including insecticides and herbicides. Its objective is to protect human health and the environment from unreasonable adverse effects of pesticides. It establishes a nationally uniform labeling system requiring the registration of all pesticides sold in the United States, and requiring users to comply with the national label. The CWA creates a comprehensive regulatory scheme to control the discharge of pollutants into the nation's waters; the discharge of pollutants without a permit violates the act.

Several federal court cases testing the relationship between FIFRA and the CWA have drawn attention since 2001. In two cases concerning pesticide applications by agriculture and natural resources managers, the U.S. Court of Appeals for the Ninth Circuit held that CWA permits are required for at least some discharges of FIFRA-regulated pesticides over, into, or near U.S. waters. It held in a third case that no permit was required for the specific pesticide in question. In 2010, the U.S. Court of Appeals for the Second Circuit ruled that a CWA discharge permit for mosquito control activities was not required before April 2011.

Several of the rulings alarmed a range of stakeholders who fear that requiring CWA permits for pesticide application activities would present significant costs, operational difficulties, and delays. Pressed to clarify its long-standing principle that CWA permits are not required for using FIFRA-approved products, EPA in 2006 issued a rule to formalize that principle in regulations. Environmental activists strongly opposed EPA's actions, arguing that FIFRA does not protect water quality from harmful pollutant discharges, as the CWA is intended to do. Other stakeholders, such as pesticide applicators, endorsed the rule. However, the rule was challenged, and in 2009, a federal court vacated the regulation. The federal government asked the court to stay the order vacating the exemption for two years, to provide time for working with states to develop a general permit for pesticide applications covered by the decision. The court denied the request for rehearing and granted the requested delay, which was extended until October 31, 2011, when EPA issued the permit. Despite the agency's efforts to minimize regulatory burdens and cost, the permit is controversial.

Some believe that the controversy will only be resolved by congressional action to clarify the intersecting scope of the Clean Water Act and FIFRA. The House passed legislation intended to nullify the 2009 federal court ruling in the 112th and 113th Congresses. Similar bills have been approved by House and Senate committees in the 114th Congress (H.R. 897, S. 659, and S. 1500). The House passed a modified version of H.R. 897, re-titled the Zika Vector Control Act, on May 24, 2016. Separate Senate legislation, S. 2899, would provide a temporary, 180-day waiver of the PGP and its reporting requirements for the purpose of public health pesticide applications of a mosquito control program.

Contents

Contacts

Introduction

It has been noted that "[t]he potential for overlapping and potentially conflicting regulatory scope between federal statutes is common, especially in the heavily regulated area of environmental protection."[1] This potential has received attention in connection with implementation of the Federal Insecticide, Fungicide, and Rodenticide Act (FIFRA)[2] and the Federal Water Pollution Control Act (Clean Water Act, CWA).[3] FIFRA requires the Environmental Protection Agency (EPA) to regulate the sale and use of pesticides in the United States through registration and labeling. The CWA is the principal federal law governing pollution in the nation's surface waters.

Pesticides used to control weeds, insects, and other pests receive public attention because of potential impacts on humans and the environment. Depending on the chemical, possible health effects from overexposure to pesticides include cancer, reproductive or nervous-system disorders, and acute toxicity. Similar effects are possible in the aquatic environment. Recent studies suggest that some pesticides can disrupt endocrine systems and affect reproduction by interfering with natural hormones.[4] However, many pesticides and their breakdown products do not have standards or guidelines, and current standards and guidelines do not yet account for exposure to mixtures and seasonal pulses of high concentrations. Effects of pesticides on aquatic life are a concern, because intensive surveys done by the U.S. Geological Survey found that more than one-half of streams sampled had concentrations of at least one pesticide that exceeded an EPA guideline for the protection of aquatic life. Whereas most toxicity and exposure assessments of pesticides are based on controlled experiments with a single contaminant, sampling by the U.S. Geological Survey found that most contamination of waterbodies occurs as pesticide mixtures.[5]

For the more than 30 years since Congress enacted FIFRA and the Clean Water Act, there had been little apparent direct conflict between them. EPA's operating principle during that time had been that pesticides used according to the requirements of FIFRA do not require regulatory consideration under the CWA. EPA had never required CWA permits for use of FIFRA-approved materials, and EPA rules did not specifically address the issue. However, EPA's interpretation and operating practice regarding the relationship between the two laws have recently been challenged in several arenas. Federal courts have been one of two battlegrounds so far where the potential conflict between the regulatory scope of these two laws has been waged. EPA regulatory proceedings have been the second battleground area. Congressional action adds a third testing of the issues.

At issue is how FIFRA-approved pesticides that are sprayed over or into waters are regulated and, specifically, whether the FIFRA regulatory regime is sufficient alone to ensure protection of water quality or whether such pesticide application requires approval under a CWA permit. The issue arose initially over challenges to some routine practices in the West (weed control in irrigation ditches and spraying for silvicultural pest control on U.S. Forest Service lands). It subsequently

---

[1] Randall S. Abate and Matthew T. Stanger, "Pesticides and Water Don't Mix: Addressing the Need to Close a Regulatory Gap Between FIFRA and the CWA," *Environmental Law Reporter News & Analysis*, January 2005, p. 10056.

[2] 7 U.S.C. §§136-136y.

[3] 33 U.S.C. §§1251-1387.

[4] For information, see CRS Report R40177, *Environmental Exposure to Endocrine Disruptors: What Are the Human Health Risks?*, by Linda-Jo Schierow and Eugene H. Buck.

[5] U.S. Department of the Interior, U.S. Geological Survey, *The Quality of Our Nation's Waters, Nutrients and Pesticides*, USGS Circular 1225, 1999, pp. 3-9.

drew more attention in connection with efforts by public health officials throughout the country to combat mosquito-borne illnesses such as West Nile virus. The litigation created uncertainty over whether application of pesticides and herbicides to waterbodies requires a water discharge permit. EPA tried to promulgate policy to clarify the relationship of the two laws and to address conflicts resulting from several judicial rulings, ultimately in a regulation issued in November 2006. That rule was challenged by multiple parties, and in January 2009, a federal appellate court vacated the rule. A related issue of interest to many pesticide applicators, but not yet addressed by EPA policy or rule, concerns pesticides that unintentionally impact waterbodies through drift or migration from nearby land, such as a field of crops.

This report provides background on the conflict over interpretation and implementation of FIFRA and the Clean Water Act. A brief discussion of the two laws is followed by a review of the major litigation of interest. EPA's efforts to clarify its policy in this area and the November 2006 rule and the 2009 federal court ruling are discussed, as well as possible options for EPA and Congress to further address the FIFRA-CWA issues. In 2011 EPA issued a general CWA permit (the Pesticide General Permit) in response to the court ruling. Despite EPA's efforts to streamline the permit and its applicability, the permit is controversial. As discussed below, Congress has for some time considered legislation to nullify the court's ruling.

The Laws

FIFRA is a regulatory statute governing the licensing, distribution, sale, and use of pesticides, including insecticides, fungicides, rodenticides, and other designated classes of chemicals. Its objective is to protect human health and the environment from unreasonable adverse effects of pesticides. To that end, it establishes a nationally uniform pesticide labeling system requiring the registration of all pesticides and herbicides sold in the United States, and requiring users to comply with conditions of use included on the national label. A FIFRA label encompasses the terms on which a chemical is registered, and its requirements become part of FIFRA's regulatory scheme. In registering the chemical, EPA makes a finding that the chemical "when used in accordance with widespread and commonly recognized practice ... will not generally cause unreasonable adverse effects on the environment" (7 U.S.C. §136a(c)(5)(D)).

EPA reviews scientific data submitted by pesticide manufacturers on toxicity and behavior in the environment to evaluate risks and exposure associated with the pesticide product's use and takes into account the costs and benefits of various pesticide uses. If a registration is granted, the agency specifies the approved uses and conditions of use, which the registrant must explain on the product label. EPA may classify and register a pesticide product for general use or for restricted use (those judged to be more dangerous to the applicator or to the environment which can only be applied by or under the direct supervision of a person who has been trained and certified). FIFRA preempts state, local, and tribal regulations stricter than or different from EPA rules with respect to labeling requirements, but allows states and localities to adopt more restrictive conditions with regard to sale and use.

Use of a pesticide product in a manner not consistent with its label is prohibited, and the law provides civil and criminal penalties for violations. Under FIFRA, EPA generally enforces the law's requirements. However, the law also gives states with adequate enforcement procedures, laws, and regulations primary authority for enforcing FIFRA provisions related to pesticide use.

The objective of the CWA is to "restore and maintain the chemical, physical, and biological integrity of the Nation's waters." To that end, it creates a comprehensive regulatory scheme to control the discharge of waste and pollutants; the discharge of pollutants into waters of the United States without a permit violates the act. The permit requirement is at the heart of the act's compliance and enforcement strategy. Several aspects of these core requirements in the law are important to evaluating whether the CWA applies to specific activities, including whether there is a discharge from a point source (a discrete conveyance such as a pipe, ditch, container, vessel, or other floating craft), whether the discharge is made into waters of the United States, and whether the material discharged is a pollutant; all of these terms are defined in the act. Especially key in the current context is whether pesticides are pollutants under the act. This issue has been central to much of the judicial and regulatory debate over whether the two laws, CWA and FIFRA, are complementary or in conflict. CWA Section 502(6) (33 U.S.C. §1362(6)) defines pollutant thus:

> The term "pollutant" means dredged spoil, solid waste, incinerator residue, sewage, garbage, sewage sludge, munitions, chemical wastes, biological materials, radioactive materials, heat, wrecked or discarded equipment, rock, sand, cellar dirt and industrial, municipal, and agricultural waste discharged into water.

Section 402 of the act establishes the National Pollutant Discharge Elimination System (NPDES) permitting requirement, which regulates the lawful discharge of pollutants. The act defines "discharge of a pollutant" to mean "any addition of any pollutant to navigable waters from any point source" (CWA §502(12); 33 U.S.C. §1362(12)). Discharges are permitted if they are authorized under a NPDES permit that meets CWA requirements, including protecting the receiving waters. NPDES permits specify limits on what pollutants may be discharged and in what amounts. They also include monitoring and reporting requirements. They are either individual case-by-case permits or general permits applicable to similar categories of activities and similar waste discharges. Under the CWA, qualified states issue NPDES permits to regulated sources and enforce permits, and the law allows states to adopt water quality requirements more stringent than federal rules. As of 2015, 46 states have been delegated authority to administer the permit program; EPA issues discharge permits in the remaining states.

The NPDES permit is the act's principal enforcement tool. EPA may issue a compliance order or bring a civil suit in U.S. district court against persons who violate the terms of a permit, and stiffer penalties are authorized for criminal violations of the act. As a practical matter, the majority of actions taken to enforce the law are undertaken by states, both because states issue the majority of permits to dischargers and because the federal government lacks the resources for day-to-day monitoring and enforcement. In addition, individuals may bring a citizen suit in U.S. district court against persons who violate the terms of a CWA-authorized permit or who discharge without a valid permit. FIFRA does not authorize citizen suits.

Throughout the United States, pesticides often are applied in, onto, or near waterbodies to control weeds and insects. Whether those pesticides are adversely affecting water quality has not been a disputed issue until recently. EPA's long-standing practice and interpretation of the laws was that a CWA permit is not required when pesticide application is done in a manner consistent with FIFRA and its regulations. But that interpretation was challenged in several lawsuits brought since the late 1990s that have been decided since 2001.

The Litigation

Five federal court cases testing the relationship between FIFRA and the CWA have drawn the most attention, three in the U.S. Court of Appeals for the Ninth Circuit in the West, concerning pesticide applications by agricultural and natural resource managers, and two in the Second Circuit Court of Appeals in the East, involving the use of pesticides by government and public health authorities for mosquito control. These cases have been brought principally under the citizen suit provisions of the CWA. Two of the Ninth Circuit decisions have held that CWA permits are required for at least some activity involving the point source discharge of FIFRA-regulated pesticides over or into waters of the United States, and the third held that a permit was not required because the specific pesticide was not a chemical waste. The Second Circuit ruled in two cases; most recently, it ruled that trucks and helicopters that discharge pesticides are point sources, but it deferred requiring permits until EPA issues a CWA general permit, which is discussed below.

The Ninth Circuit Cases

The first of the major cases on these issues involved application of herbicides in irrigation ditches. In the case, a major issue was whether the application of pesticides constitutes the discharge of a pollutant. Environmental groups challenged application of an aquatic herbicide called Magnicide H to kill weeds and algae and sought to require that the applicator, a municipal corporation that operates a system of irrigation canals in Oregon, obtain an NPDES permit.

The U.S. Court of Appeals for the Ninth Circuit endorsed the lower court's ruling that the pesticide was a pollutant under the CWA, and that the irrigation canals into which the pesticide was being sprayed are "waters of the United States."[6] But it rejected the lower court's holding that a CWA permit was not required because the pesticide was properly regulated by FIFRA and had an EPA-approved FIFRA label. The appeals court ruled that FIFRA and CWA have different purposes and that, as such, neither could be controlling on the application of the other. The court said that FIFRA creates a comprehensive regulatory scheme for the labeling of pesticides, requiring that all insecticides and herbicides sold in the United States be registered with the EPA. It and the CWA have different, although complementary, purposes, the court said, and using a pesticide with a FIFRA-approved label does not obviate the need to obtain a CWA permit. The FIFRA label is the same nationwide. The CWA permit considers local environmental conditions, which the FIFRA label does not. Thus, a nationwide label on a FIFRA-regulated chemical could not be controlling on whether a CWA permit is required, because it does not account for location-specific requirements. The court reversed the district court's grant of summary judgment in favor of the defendants.[7]

Several of the states within the Ninth Circuit subsequently took actions to respond to this ruling. California and Washington amended their water quality program rules to require NPDES permits for pesticide applicators. Oregon did not mandate permits, but suggested that pesticide applicators obtain state-issued permits to protect against lawsuits. Other states outside of the Ninth Circuit have continued their long-standing practice of not issuing permits to persons who apply pesticides to waters of the United States.

The second major case in the West involved an annual U.S. Forest Service (USFS) aerial spray program over national forest lands in Oregon and Washington. Environmental groups filed a lawsuit challenging the spraying program, saying that the environmental impact statement (EIS) prepared by the USFS was inadequate and that the Forest Service had failed to obtain a CWA permit, which they argued is required for this type of aerial spraying. The appeals court reversed the district court's grant of summary judgment for the Forest Service and instructed the lower court to enter an injunction prohibiting the federal agency from further spraying until it acquires

---

[6] In view of the Supreme Court's June 2006 decision in *Rapanos v. United States* (547 U.S. 715, 2006), coverage of irrigation canals as "waters of the United States" may depend on case-specific circumstances, because the Court's plurality opinion in this case made specific reference to *Headwaters, Inc. v. Talent Irrigation District*. For additional information, see CRS Report RL33263, *The Wetlands Coverage of the Clean Water Act (CWA): Rapanos and Beyond*, by Robert Meltz and Claudia Copeland.

[7] Headwaters, Inc. v. Talent Irrigation District, 243 F.3d 526 (9th Cir. 2001).

an NPDES permit and completes a revised EIS.[8] The court disagreed with the argument of the Forest Service that the spraying is nonpoint source water pollution, which does not require an NPDES permit. The court held that the insecticides meet the CWA definition of "pollutant" and that the application came from an aircraft equipped with spraying apparatus, thus meeting all of the elements of the CWA's definition of point source pollution.

In September 2003, the EPA General Counsel issued a legal memorandum to officials in states located in the Ninth Circuit responding to the *Forsgren* case. The memorandum said that EPA disagreed with the court's holding in the case and that outside the Ninth Circuit, EPA would continue its long-standing interpretation of FIFRA and the CWA. Within the Ninth Circuit, the memo said, EPA would not acquiesce to the ruling in the case of materials other than pesticides (such as those used for fire control), or in circumstances where pesticides are not applied directly over and into waters of the United States.[9]

The third Ninth Circuit case involved an effort by the Montana Department of Fish, Wildlife and Parks to intentionally apply the pesticide antimycin to a river in order to remove non-native trout species and thus to allow re-introducing a threatened fish species into the river. The director of the department was sued under the citizen suit provision of the CWA by a citizen who sought to require the department to obtain an NPDES permit before applying the pesticide.

The court held in this instance that no NPDES permit was required, because the facts of the case demonstrated that, following application as intended, the antimycin dissipated rapidly, leaving no excess portions or residual chemical that should be characterized as chemical waste, and thus is not a pollutant under the act.[10] Intentionally applied and properly performing pesticides are not pollutants, the court said.

The court distinguished this case from its ruling in *Headwaters*, saying that the factual scenarios differ, because "in that case the 'chemical waste' for which a NPDES permit was required was not a pesticide serving a beneficial purpose and intentionally applied to water, but was a chemical that remained in the water after the Magnicide H performed its intended, beneficial function."[11] Further, the court stated that its analysis accords with EPA's construction of the CWA's definition of "chemical waste" in the context of intentionally applied pesticides, and that the agency's 2003 Interim Statement and Guidance addressing the issue (discussed below) is entitled to some deference. EPA's interpretation as presented in that Interim Statement is reasonable and not in conflict with the expressed intent of Congress, the court said.

The Second Circuit Cases

Two cases in the U.S. Court of Appeals for the Second Circuit involved the use of pesticides for mosquito control. In the first case, several residents of the Town of Amherst, NY, sought to halt aerial application of pesticides without a CWA permit. The district court initially dismissed the case, stating that spray drift is not chemical waste under the CWA and that the pesticide use was best regulated under FIFRA. But the appeals court remanded the case to the district court for

---

[8] League of Wilderness Defenders/Blue Mountains Biodiversity Project v. Forsgren, 309 F.3d 1181 (9th Cir. 2002).

[9] Robert Fabricant, EPA General Counsel, "Interpretive Statement and Guidance Addressing Effect of Ninth Circuit Decision in *League of Wilderness Defenders v. Forsgren* on Application of Pesticides and Fire Retardants," memorandum, September 3, 2003, 7 pp.

[10] Fairhurst v. Hagener, 422 F.3d 1146 (9th Cir. 2005).

[11] Ibid. at 1150.

further development of the record.[12] Although this ruling may not be cited as precedent, it is notable in that, while EPA had filed an *amicus curiae* brief providing its views on this particular case, the court invited EPA to offer its views broadly on the policy and legal questions. The court stated:

> Until the EPA articulates a clear interpretation of current law—among other things, whether properly used pesticides released into or over waters of the United States can trigger the requirement for NPDES permits ...—the question of whether properly used pesticides can become pollutants that violate the CWA will remain open. Participation by the EPA in this litigation in any way that permits articulation of the EPA's interpretation of the law in this situation would be of great assistance to the courts.[13]

The second pertinent case in the Second Circuit also involved the use of pesticides for control of mosquitoes. Plaintiffs in the case, a citizens group, sought an injunction to halt the aerial and ground spraying, arguing that although the pesticides were properly regulated under FIFRA, the spraying program involved the discharge of a pollutant without a CWA permit, and thus was a violation of that law. A federal district court held that FIFRA-compliant spraying activity did not amount to the discharge of a pollutant into navigable waters from a point source, and thus did not violate the CWA. In March 2010, the Second Circuit Court of Appeals disagreed with the district court's finding that trucks and helicopters were not "point source," which are required to have CWA permits in order to discharge lawfully, but this court held that no permits would be required for the challenged activities until EPA issues a general permit, as it did in 2011 (see discussion below, "Options for EPA").[14]

Other Litigation

Other lawsuits have followed these cases. For example, private citizens who operate an organic fruit farm in Gem County, Idaho, brought suit against the local mosquito abatement district there, seeking to require a CWA permit for pesticide spraying. Finding itself in the proverbial spot "between a rock and a hard place," the mosquito abatement district applied for a permit from EPA, which the agency declined to issue, based on its long-standing policy and legal interpretation. Thereafter, the mosquito abatement district filed a lawsuit against EPA in an attempt to obtain a declaration that a CWA permit is not needed and to avoid the citizen suit litigation, which is pending in federal court in Idaho. The mosquito abatement district asked the federal court either for a judgment saying that no permit is required or, if the court were to determine otherwise, an order directing EPA to process its CWA permit application. In January 2005, the federal district court in the District of Columbia dismissed the case because the mosquito abatement district and EPA were in agreement that no CWA permit is required for pesticide applications that are consistent with FIFRA.[15]

In other locations, citizen groups have given notice, as required by the CWA, of possible lawsuits to expand the precedent from the Ninth Circuit cases to other types of operations. For example, two actions were threatened against Maine blueberry farmers for failing to obtain a CWA permit for spraying pesticides that may drift off-target from land into waterbodies. In response to the litigation pressure, however, both farmers subsequently announced plans to cease aerial spraying and instead rely on ground spraying, until such time as government or the courts clarify the law.

---

[12] Altman v. Town of Amherst, N.Y., 47 Fed. Appx. 62 (2d Cir. 2002).

[13] 47 Fed. Appx. at 67.

[14] Peconic Baykeeper Inc. v. Suffolk County, 2d Cir., No. 09-97-cv, March 30, 2010.

[15] Gem County Mosquito Abatement District v. EPA, 398 F. Supp. 2d 1 (D.D.C. 2005)

EPA's Regulatory Responses: 2003-2006

The rulings by the Ninth Circuit in the *Talent* and *Forsgren* cases and possible endorsement by other courts greatly alarmed a range of stakeholders in the regulated community, including forestry, agriculture, and pesticide applicators, as well as municipal and public health officials concerned with the need to control mosquitoes and other vectors associated with diseases such as West Nile virus and malaria. They feared that CWA permit requirements would be extended to agricultural and other activities that have not traditionally been regulated under the CWA. They argue that if permits tailored to particular circumstances are deemed necessary, such requirements would present significant costs, operational difficulties, and delays to applicators. They also would put pressure on limited federal and state CWA permitting resources. In their view, requiring permits will not be environmentally helpful, but the expense and long delays of permitting proceedings will hamper programs that are needed for controlling pests that threaten public health and crops. In response, EPA issued two interpretive guidance documents (in 2003 and 2005) and in 2005 proposed a rulemaking to formalize its long-standing position on CWA-FIFRA issues. A final rule was promulgated in November 2006 but was vacated by a federal court in 2009, as discussed below.

EPA Guidance

After the *Altman v. Town of Amherst* ruling in 2002, industry, states, and others, including some in Congress, pressed EPA to clarify the emerging conflicts over the two laws. EPA responded with a guidance document in 2005.[16] The agency's consistent position, expressed in the guidance, was that pesticides applied in a manner consistent with FIFRA do not constitute either chemical wastes or biological materials under the definition of pollutant in Section 502(6) of the CWA. The rationale for this position was that it is consistent with over 30 years of CWA administration. At the same time, EPA said that pesticide applications in violation of FIFRA, that is, when not used or applied according to applicable labeling requirements, would be subject to all relevant statutes, including the Clean Water Act.

Environmental activists strongly objected to EPA's position in the guidance, which they viewed as contrary to the judicial rulings. These groups reiterated points made by the Ninth Circuit court in the *Headwaters* and *Forsgren* rulings, namely that chemical and biological pesticides are pollutants within the meaning of the CWA, because the law defines pollutants broadly and includes, among other substances, chemical wastes, biological materials, and agricultural wastes. As that court has declared, environmentalists said, FIFRA does not override the CWA, and the two statutes must work in tandem to prevent injury to aquatic life. They also argued that EPA was wrongly deciding that materials with beneficial uses should not be construed as pollutants under the CWA.

Environmentalists' objections also went to the policy problems of relying on FIFRA to protect water quality from pesticide applications, as that would be the result of EPA's position. That position, critics said, turns on whether the pesticide application conforms procedurally with FIFRA requirements, not what is the water quality impact of that pesticide. Other concerns raised by critics included the fact that while the FIFRA registration process calls for ecological risk assessment that may be adequate for producing nationally applicable labels, it does not ensure that local water quality standards are maintained and does not account for additive or synergistic

---

[16] U.S. Environmental Protection Agency, "Application of Pesticides to Waters of the United States in Compliance With FIFRA, proposed rulemaking and notice of interpretive statement," 70 *Federal Register* 5093, February 1, 2005.

effects of multiple pollutants discharged to a particular waterbody. Environmentalists argued that the CWA provides the means to determine whether, and under what conditions, it is safe to discharge a particular pesticide into a particular body of water, and that FIFRA's nationally uniform labeling system cannot do that. FIFRA is not specifically charged with ensuring the chemical, physical, and biological integrity of U.S. waterways, and satisfaction of a pesticide's FIFRA labeling criteria does not automatically satisfy water quality concerns, as the NPDES permit process is intended to do. They also maintained that FIFRA fails to consider the lasting effects that pesticide residues have on a local ecosystem and that localized analysis of the environmental impact of pollutant discharges under the CWA is necessary, due to the toxic residues that remain after pesticide application, which FIFRA does not address.

Industry welcomed the thrust of the EPA guidance but also urged that it be broadened. Agricultural groups requested that EPA include other classes of applications under the guidance, such as aquaculture and crop production. Beyond the types of uses described in the guidance, some argued that EPA should additionally clarify that CWA permits are not required in the case of pesticides that are applied over land and then inadvertently impact waterbodies through drift and migration. Many requested that EPA address the issues definitively in a rulemaking, rather than in non-binding guidance. In their view, without clear regulatory language supporting EPA's interpretation, pesticide applicators would still face the prospect of citizen lawsuits and NPDES permit requirements.

Many states and local governments, including agriculture agencies, irrigation districts, and mosquito abatement districts, strongly endorsed EPA's proposed clarification of its interpretation of the two laws. However, a few—especially states located in the jurisdiction of the federal Ninth Circuit—expressed a different view. The Oregon Department of Environmental Quality and California State Water Resources Control Board commented that the Interim Statement conflicted with legal precedent in the *Headwaters* case. They urged EPA, if it wishes to create an exemption for pesticide applications conducted in compliance with FIFRA, to ask Congress to amend the Clean Water Act and FIFRA accordingly.

Regulatory Proposal

At the same time that it issued the 2005 guidance, EPA proposed a rulemaking to codify the substance of the guidance in CWA regulations, which it promulgated in November 2006.[17] The rule added two specific circumstances that would be excluded from NPDES permit requirements, when the application complies with relevant requirements of FIFRA:

- the application of pesticides directly to waters of the United States in order to control pests (e.g., to control mosquito larvae or aquatic weeds); and

- the application of pesticides to control pests that are present over waters of the United States, including near such waters, where a portion of the pesticides will unavoidably be deposited to waters of the United States in order to target the pests effectively.

In the rule, EPA provided a lengthy discussion of its rationale that pesticides, when applied pursuant to FIFRA, are not chemical wastes or biological materials and thus are not what the CWA defines as "pollutants" (see discussion, page 3). However, EPA also acknowledged that application of pesticides may leave residual materials in U.S. waters after the product has served

---

[17] U.S. Environmental Protection Agency, "Application of Pesticides to Waters of the United States in Compliance With FIFRA," Final Rule, 71 *Federal Register* 68483, November 27, 2006.

its beneficial purpose and that these residual materials may be "pollutants" under the act at that later time. Nonetheless, even in such cases, EPA said, the initial application of the pesticide does not require an NPDES permit because EPA does not consider it to be a pollutant *at the time of its discharge* into water.[18] The agency also responded to some public comments that had criticized the adequacy of FIFRA's registration process for consideration of water quality, local conditions, etc. EPA said that the "regulatory and non-regulatory tools under FIFRA provide means of addressing water quality problems arising from the use of pesticides," particularly the registration and re-registration processes, which consider both human health and aquatic resource impacts.[19]

Judicial Challenge to the EPA Rule

The 2006 rule prompted multiple lawsuits by industry and environmental groups in almost every judicial circuit nationwide. The litigation was consolidated in the Sixth Circuit Court of Appeals. Industry's challenge argued that the rule was arbitrary and capricious because it treated pesticides applied in violation of FIFRA as pollutants, while treating the same pesticides used in compliance with FIFRA as non-pollutants. It also sought to expand the rule to apply to all pesticides and all agricultural applications of pesticides, including applications to land that drift over or into water. Environmentalists' challenge claimed that, by exempting FIFRA-compliant applications of pesticides from CWA requirements, EPA ignored its duties under the Clean Water Act.

The court's ruling was issued January 7, 2009.[20] EPA had argued that at the time of discharge, a pesticide is a non-pollutant. Excess pesticide or pesticide residues do not exist until after the discharge is complete, EPA said, and therefore should be treated as nonpoint source pollutants that do not require CWA permits. The court rejected EPA's attempt to "inject[] a temporal requirement to the 'discharge of a pollutant,'" and it said that such an interpretation is unsupported by the CWA, and is also contrary to the purpose of the permitting program. The court said, "If the EPA's interpretation were allowed to stand, discharges that are innocuous at the time they are made but extremely harmful at a later point would not be subject to the permitting program." It concluded that "there is no room for the EPA's argument that residual and excess pesticides do not require an NPDES permit," and the court thus vacated the rule. The vacatur was scheduled to take effect April 9, 2009, but subsequently the Sixth Circuit granted the government's request to delay the effective date of the ruling for two years, so that EPA could develop a regulatory response, as discussed below. In the meantime, the rule remains in effect.[21]

In February 2010, the Supreme Court declined to review the Sixth Circuit's ruling.

Initial Congressional Interest and Options

Congressional interest in these issues became apparent after the first federal appeals court ruling in the 2001 *Headwaters v. Talent* ruling. Two congressional hearings focused on implications of the cases for pesticide use generally and for local governments' efforts to control mosquito-borne illnesses such as West Nile Virus. Also, a hearing also was held on legislation introduced in the

---

[18] Id. at 68487.

[19] Id. at 68488-68489.

[20] National Cotton Council of America v. U.S. Environmental Protection Agency, 553 F.3d 927 (6th Cir. 2009).

[21] On June 27, 2013, EPA promulgated a rule to remove the NPDES permit exemption, vacated by the Sixth Circuit in 2009, from CWA regulations. U.S. Environmental Protection Agency, "National Pollutant Discharge Elimination system Regulation Revision: Removal of the Pesticide Discharge Permitting Exemption in Response to Sixth Circuit Court of Appeals Decision, Final Rule," 78 *Federal Register* 38591-38594, June 27, 2013.

109th Congress to clarify the scope of the CWA regarding the use of FIFRA-approved pesticides, fire retardants, and biological control organisms.

The first of these hearings was in October 2002, when a House Transportation and Infrastructure subcommittee held a fact-finding hearing on the issues.[22] The subcommittee's particular concern derived in part from the fact that one of the key practices used to manage stormwater runoff, which is regulated under the Clean Water Act, is to collect and hold it in retention ponds, basins, drainage ditches, etc. Such practices can be at odds with the public health objective of controlling insect-breeding habitat by eliminating or draining sources of standing water. Stormwater management practices typically allow collected water to drain slowly, while public health efforts would prefer that it be removed quickly. Another way to address the public health concerns is to spray pesticides on stormwater management structures and other areas of standing waters. The question for this subcommittee was the uncertainty raised by the litigation over the CWA-FIFRA issues for communities, industries, and others needing to maintain stormwater control systems. An EPA official, while acknowledging that the issue of CWA jurisdiction over pesticide spraying is "new territory" for the agency, said that EPA believed there is no inherent conflict between protecting water quality and preventing mosquito-borne disease. At the hearing, some Members and witnesses urged EPA to provide guidance to resolve uncertainties raised by the court rulings.

The second congressional hearing, held by a House Government Reform subcommittee in October 2004, examined challenges to controlling West Nile Virus.[23] The hearing was an opportunity for some Members and witnesses to express the view that EPA's July 2003 interim guidance, while helpful in clarifying EPA's position, failed to resolve all legal uncertainty, since it would not bind non-federal entities or bar citizen lawsuits. Witnesses said that EPA's guidance is a nonbinding legal document that would not deter filing of citizen lawsuits seeking to impose a permit requirement. Supporters of this view urged EPA to settle the legal questions through a formal rulemaking to revise CWA rules. An EPA official said that even if EPA were to promulgate a rule (as it subsequently did), states will still have the discretion to continue to require non-NPDES permits, and a formal rule would not preclude citizen lawsuits from seeking to force localities to file for permits. EPA acknowledged these same points in the 2005 guidance. Others at this hearing agreed on the need for a formal rulemaking, but recommended that in doing so, EPA should reverse the interpretation detailed in the guidance, not codify it.

In the 108th Congress, Senate appropriators included language in their report on EPA's FY2005 funding bill calling on EPA to finalize the interim guidance by December 2004 and to clarify the long-standing distinction between agriculture and silviculture activities that do and do not require CWA permits.[24]

In 2003, a number of House and Senate Members urged the Bush Administration to support Supreme Court review of the *Forsgren* case, but ultimately the Administration did not endorse industry's request for a review, and the Court did not grant certiorari. Some Members of Congress

---

[22] U.S. Congress, House, Committee on Transportation and Infrastructure, Subcommittee on Water Resources and Environment, "West Nile Virus: The Clean Water Act and Mosquito Control," Hearing, October 10, 2002, 107th Cong., 2nd sess., unpublished.

[23] U.S. Congress, House, Committee on Government Reform, Subcommittee on Energy Policy, Natural Resources and Regulatory Affairs, "Current Challenges in Controlling the West Nile Virus," Hearing, October 6, 2004, 108th Cong., 2nd sess. (Serial No. 108-274), 182 pp.

[24] U.S. Senate, Committee on Appropriations, "Departments of Veterans Affairs and Housing and Urban Development, and Independent Agencies Appropriations Bill, 2005," report to accompany S. 2825, 108th Cong., 2nd sess., pp. 110-111.

also submitted comments in support of the July 2003 interim guidance document and the January 2005 regulatory proposal.

Options for EPA

As described above, in January 2009, the U.S. Sixth Circuit Court of Appeals rejected EPA's rationale for its 2006 rule that attempted to specify circumstances in which pesticides applied to waters of the United States do not require NPDES permits. The court appeared to leave little room for EPA to fashion a new rule consistent with the agency's long-standing view that FIFRA-compliant applications do not require CWA permits. Agriculture industry groups were fearful that the court's ruling would lead to permit requirements for each pesticide application, placing significant burdens on industry and EPA. Accordingly, several industry groups (the American Farm Bureau Federation, American Forest and Paper Association, and CropLife America, the trade organization for agriculture and pest management) petitioned for a rehearing of the case by the full Sixth Circuit court, but the rehearing request was rejected.

The federal government did not seek a rehearing of the case. Instead, the government petitioned the court for a two-year stay of the order vacating the exemption, to give EPA time to work with states and the regulated community to develop a general permit for pesticide applications covered by the decision. State water pollution agencies supported the government's request for the two-year delay, which the court granted.

EPA's Pesticide General Permit

The two basic types of NPDES permits are individual permits that are specifically tailored for an individual discharger, and general permits that cover categories of point sources having common elements and that discharge the same types of wastes. General permits allow the permitting authority to allocate resources efficiently, especially when there is potentially a large number of permittees, and to provide timely permit coverage. Both individual and general permits are enforceable by the permitting authority and by private citizens (in federal court).

EPA uses its authority to issue NPDES general permits frequently, such as a general permit to cover discharges incidental to the normal operation of vessels (Vessel General Permit, or VGP) that applies to approximately 69,000 vessels.[25] Typically, dischargers seeking coverage under a general permit are required to submit a notice of intent to be covered by the permit, but this can be modified. For example, in the VGP, EPA provided automatic coverage for about 20,000 of the covered vessels. Still, even with general permits, development and implementation issues arise, including how EPA specifies applicable discharge limits based on technology available to treat pollutant constituents found in the discharge (i.e., effluent limits), and limits that are protective of the designated uses of the impacted water (i.e., water quality-based effluent limits), as required by the CWA.

EPA issued the pesticide general permit on October 31, 2011, as required by the federal court.[26] EPA estimates that the universe of activities affected by the court's ruling is approximately 5.6 million applications annually, which are performed by 365,000 applicators, including mosquito

---

[25] For information on this general permit, see CRS Report R42142, *EPA's Vessel General Permits: Background and Issues*, by Claudia Copeland.

[26] U.S. Environmental Protection Agency, "Final National Pollutant Discharge Elimination System (NPDES) Pesticide General Permit for Point Source Discharges From the Application of Pesticides; Notice of final permit," 76 *Federal Register* 68750-68756, November 7, 2011.

and other flying insect pest control, aquatic weed and algae control, aquatic nuisance animal control, and forest canopy pest control. The permit covers about 500 different pesticide active ingredients that are contained in approximately 3,700 product labels.

The permit applies to a variety of entities, including agricultural interests involved in crop and timber tract production, forest nurseries, and operating irrigation systems; pesticide and agricultural chemical manufacturing; mosquito or other vector control districts and commercial applicators that service them; utilities (e.g., electric power, natural gas, water supply and wastewater); and government agencies and departments engaged in air and water resource management and conservation. It requires all operators to minimize pesticide discharges to waters by practices such as using the lowest effect amount of pesticide product that is optimal for controlling the target pest. It also requires operators to prepare pesticide discharge management plans to document their pest management practices. Permittees must monitor for observable adverse effects in the treatment area and where the pesticides are discharged to U.S. waters.

The permit does not cover agricultural stormwater runoff or irrigation return flow, as these discharges are statutorily exempt from CWA permitting, and it also does not cover terrestrial application to control pests on agricultural crops or forest floors (i.e., it would not apply to pesticide applications that do not result in a discharge to U.S. waters). The EPA general permit applies in states and areas where EPA is the NPDES permitting authority, but it is being used as a model for other states to develop their own general permits.[27]

Issuance of the final permit was delayed several times and for several reasons: time needed to complete consultations with federal resource agencies under the Endangered Species Act (ESA); time needed for non-federal permitting authorities to review the final permit; and time needed by EPA to develop an electronic system on the Internet to accommodate permit applications.

In response to a number of commenters, EPA made certain changes in the final permit from the June 2010 proposal. While it covers the same pesticide use patterns as in the draft (mosquitoes and other flying insects, weed and algae control, animal pest control, and forest canopy pest control), the final permit increases the acreage threshold for requirements to submit a NOI to a permitting authority. For example, the draft stated that pesticides used to control mosquitoes or other flying insect pests would be subject to the NOI requirement if applied to 640 acres or more annually. Under the final permit, that threshold was increased to 6,400 acres per calendar year.

The final permit includes Endangered Species Act (ESA) provisions, following consultation with the National Oceanic and Atmospheric Administration (NOAA) Fisheries Service. As a result, coverage under the permit is available only for discharges not likely to adversely affect species that are listed as endangered or threatened under the ESA.[28]

Draft 2016 PGP

The 2011 PGP will expire on October 31, 2016, and in anticipation of that date, on January 26, EPA proposed a draft general PGP to replace the one that will expire. EPA said that the draft permit has the same applicability, conditions, and requirements as the 2011 permit. The 2016 permit will take effect in the same states, U.S. territories, Indian lands, and federal facilities as the

---

[27] The CWA authorizes EPA to delegate NPDES permitting authority to qualified states, and EPA has done so for the majority of states. For this permit, EPA is the permitting authority in Massachusetts, New Mexico, New Hampshire, Oklahoma, Alaska, Idaho, and the District of Columbia; Indian lands in all states except Maine; all U.S. territories except the Virgin Islands; and at federal facilities in Delaware, Vermont, Colorado, and Washington.

[28] For information, see CRS Report RL31654, *The Endangered Species Act: A Primer*, by M. Lynne Corn.

2011 permit; states will issue their own NPDES permits for pesticide discharges in the other states. Public comments on the draft permit were accepted until March 11, 2016. The EPA asked for comment on costs incurred by permit holders, but said that its estimates show a minimal burden.[29]

Other EPA Options

One issue that EPA could address separately, in addition to developing a general NPDES permit, is pesticide drift, that is, pesticide particles and droplets that migrate from the application area, which can affect people's health and the environment, as well as damage nearby crops. The *Federal Register* Notice accompanying the 2006 rule had noted that, at the time, EPA was awaiting advice from a workgroup of its Pesticide Program Dialogue Committee, which could recommend further actions. This committee was established in 1995 as a forum to provide feedback to EPA on various pesticide regulatory, policy, and program implementation issues. It is authorized pursuant to the Federal Advisory Committee Act (FACA), which details requirements for the management and oversight of federal advisory committees to ensure impartial and relevant expertise and advice to EPA and other agencies. In 2006, the committee convened a Spray Drift Workgroup charged with studying the issue of pesticide drift across water and its accompanying impact on water quality and wildlife. The following year, the workgroup finalized a report that focused on issues related to product labeling, applicator training, and practices and equipment to mitigate drift and adverse effects. In 2009, EPA proposed new pesticide labels to reduce the drifting of spray and dust from pesticide applications. The agency also has proposed several guidance documents addressing pesticide spray drift, including guidance for pesticide labeling and guidance on how off-site spray drift will be evaluated for ecological, drinking water, and human health risk assessments. In 2014, EPA announced a voluntary Drift Reduction Technology program under which manufacturers of spraying devices may conduct studies of their products to see how much drift they prevent. EPA will then assign a rating, based on how much spray drift is reduced by the device.

Other options for EPA relate to implementation of FIFRA and procedures used to evaluate the risks of pesticides during the registration process. Environmentalists have argued for some time that EPA's risk review procedures are inadequate because they fail to account for synergistic and additive effects, as well as sub-lethal and indirect effects of pollutants on the environment. In 2003, EPA convened a task force of officials from its pesticide and water quality offices to explore, among other things, whether the agency's pesticide review processes are protective enough to meet water quality standard limits. One outcome of the task force's review could be changes to implementation of FIFRA in order to address some of these concerns. Subsequently, EPA officials held a series of regional meetings with state pesticide and water quality agencies and other stakeholders and announced plans to complete a series of white papers on how to harmonize methods used by the agency's Office of Water and the Office of Pesticide Programs for ecological assessment of pesticide chemicals' water quality risks. The white papers are intended to address what officials acknowledge is a gap between the way the CWA and FIFRA approach pesticide risk and to support a consistent and common set of effects characterization methods using best available information.

---

[29] U.S. Environmental Protection Agency, "Draft National Pollutant Discharge Elimination System (NPDES) Pesticide General Permit for Point Source Discharges From the Application of Pesticides; Reissuance," 81 *Federal Register* 4289-4294, January 26, 2016.

Congressional Activity

Prior to the 2009 federal court ruling that vacated EPA's rule, some environmental activists favored legislation to clarify that NPDES permits *are* required, since they contended that the rule was unlawful. However, no such legislation was introduced. Others argued during this time that legislation is not needed because, in their view, the CWA is clear enough that permits are required for discharge of pesticides from point sources. The federal court's review of the EPA rule supports that view. But, following the court's ruling, other stakeholders came to favor legislation to support a narrow view of the CWA's jurisdiction on this issue. Although many acknowledge that any such legislative effort would be controversial and could be seen as representing not clarification but, rather, an environmental rollback, lawmakers in the House and Senate have repeatedly attempted to pass such a bill.

Legislation intended to clarify that permits are not required for some or all pesticide spraying activity was first introduced in the 109th Congress (H.R. 1749 and S. 1269, the Pest Management and Fire Suppression Flexibility Act). These bills would have provided that NPDES permits are not required for the use of FIFRA-approved pesticides; chemicals, fire retardants, or water used for fire suppression; biological organisms used for plant pest or weed control; or silviculture activities such as timber harvesting that are not currently regulated as point source activities.

As discussed above, EPA's 2006 rule (although subsequently vacated by a federal court) addressed situations in which pesticides are put directly in waters to control pests (e.g., controlling mosquito larvae or aquatic weeds) or cases of pesticides that are present over water and a portion of the pesticide is deposited in the water (e.g., aerial application to a forest canopy where waters of the United States may be present below the canopy) and excluded these situations from requiring a CWA permit. The proposed legislation in the 109th Congress, in addition to codifying these policies, also would have addressed other, broader circumstances that EPA had declined to include in the rule: applications over land areas that may drift over and into waters of the United States, broad exemption of activities for preventing or controlling plant pests or noxious weeds, and use of fire retardants.

In 2005, a House Transportation and Infrastructure subcommittee held a hearing on H.R. 1749.[30] Witnesses representing a number of sectors that are pesticide users (state foresters, western irrigation districts, and farmers) testified in support of the legislation, saying that it would resolve existing legal uncertainties about permitting. An EPA witness said that the agency's then-proposed rulemaking was intended to reduce uncertainty about the relationship between FIFRA and the CWA. The EPA official did not expressly endorse the legislation, but he said that EPA appreciated congressional efforts to reduce potential confusion over these issues. There was no further action on either H.R. 1749 or S. 1269 during the 109th Congress, and no similar bills were introduced in the 110th Congress.

Legislation on this issue was introduced in the 111th Congress. One proposal was contained in identical bills, S. 3735 and H.R. 6087. The intention of the these bills was similar to that of the earlier bills—to clarify permitting requirements under other laws and, effectively, to nullify the 2009 federal court ruling—but the 111th Congress legislation differed in several respects. First, it would have amended FIFRA, while the earlier bills would have amended the CWA. Second, the bills would not expressly have exempted chemicals, fire retardants, water used for fire

---

[30] U.S. Congress, House, Committee on Transportation and Infrastructure, Subcommittee on Water Resources and Environment, "Hearing, 'H.R. 1749, Pest Management and Fire Suppression Flexibility Act,'" 109th Cong., 1st sess., September 29, 2005 (109-33), 110 pp.

suppression, or specified silviculture activities from permit requirements. Third, S. 3735 and H.R. 6087 were broader in their potential application. The earlier bills were limited to exempting FIFRA-authorized activities from CWA permits, but the 111th Congress legislation would have exempted FIFRA-authorized activities from permits required by other federal environmental laws (including the CWA), other federal non-environmental permits or licenses, as well as state or local laws and ordinances. Pursuant to authority in FIFRA, many state and local governments control pesticide application within their jurisdictions by employing permitting systems to restrict aerial application of pesticides, or by imposing notice-and-posting requirements.

Another bill in the 111th Congress was H.R. 6273. This bill also was intended to nullify the 2009 federal court ruling, but it was narrower in scope than the other two measures. It would have amended both FIFRA and the CWA to provide that a CWA permit shall not be required by EPA, nor shall EPA require a state to require a permit, for the application of any pesticide that is subject to FIFRA if it is applied in conformance with that act.

112th and 113th Congresses

Attention to these issues resumed in the 112th Congress, because the PGP has remained controversial. Critics continue to argue that requirements of CWA and FIFRA are duplicative, although others disagree, saying that the purposes and approaches of the two laws differ greatly (see discussion of "The Laws" above). Even as they are beginning to implement permit requirements for pesticide discharges, water quality officials in some states have said that they see little water quality benefit from the permit. Despite EPA's contention that many farms are not affected by the *National Cotton Council* ruling and do not need CWA permits for their pesticide applications,[31] the PGP has been particularly controversial in the agriculture community.

At a joint hearing of subcommittees of the House Agriculture and Transportation and Infrastructure committees in February 2011, draft legislation to overturn the *National Cotton Council* ruling was discussed. Subsequently introduced as H.R. 872, the bill would amend FIFRA and the CWA to provide that neither EPA nor a state may require a CWA permit for discharge of a pesticide whose use has been authorized pursuant to FIFRA. The bill defined specified circumstances where a permit would be required (e.g., municipal or industrial treatment works effluent that contains pesticide or pesticide residue). At the hearing, some Members indicated that the bill had been drafted with EPA's technical assistance, but the Administration's official position on H.R. 872 was unknown.

The House passed H.R. 872 on March 31, 2011, by a vote of 292-130. The Senate Committee on Agriculture, Nutrition, and Forestry approved the bill without amendment in June 2011. The text of H.R. 872 also was included as a provision of H.R. 2584, a bill providing FY2012 appropriations for EPA, which the House debated in July 2011, without taking final action.

Related bills in the 112th Congress included S. 3605 (similar to H.R. 872, with the addition of a report to Congress on effectiveness of regulatory actions related to pesticide registration and protecting water quality) and S. 718 (a bill to amend only FIFRA to clarify that, notwithstanding any other law, no permit shall be required for use of a FIFRA-registered pesticide or organisms or practices covered by the Plant Protection Act).

In July 2012, the House Agriculture Committee ordered reported the 2012 farm bill (H.R. 6083, the Federal Agriculture Reform and Risk Management Act). A provision identical to House-

---

[31] U.S. Environmental Protection Agency, "Information on the Pesticide General Permit for Agricultural Stakeholders," December 2011, http://www.epa.gov/npdes/pubs/pgp_agfactsheet.pdf.

passed H.R. 872 was included in the legislation. The Senate had previously passed its version of a 2012 farm bill (S. 3240); it did not include a similar provision. The 112ᵗʰ Congress did not take final action on comprehensive farm bill legislation.

Legislation to nullify the 2009 federal court ruling also was introduced in the 113ᵗʰ Congress (H.R. 935, similar to H.R. 872 in the 112ᵗʰ Congress; S. 175, similar to S. 718 in the 112ᵗʰ Congress; and S. 802, similar to S. 3605 in the 112ᵗʰ Congress). The House passed H.R. 935 on July 31, 2014, by a vote of 267-161.

In addition, a provision similar to H.R. 935 was included in farm bill legislation approved by the House in June 2013 (H.R. 2642). However, the Senate-passed version of farm bill renewal legislation (S. 954) did not include a similar provision. The 2014 farm bill, enacted in February 2014 (the Agricultural Act of 2014, P.L. 113-79), also did not include a provision to overturn the Sixth Circuit ruling.

114ᵗʰ Congress

The PGP requirements have been in place for nearly five years. In March 2015, an EPA official stated during congressional testimony that the agency is not aware of any issues with the permit or of any instances of individuals not being able to apply a pesticide in a timely manner. Further, EPA is not aware of any active litigation in connection with the PGP.

Nevertheless, it remains controversial. Critics of the permit continue to argue that its CWA requirements are duplicative of FIFRA and are burdensome, due to costs that applicators incur in obtaining permits. Critics also say that applicators are vulnerable to potential CWA citizen suit litigation. Supporters of the permit respond that the two laws are different because the CWA allows evaluation of pesticides' impacts on localized waterbodies, while FIFRA makes more generalized determination of impacts on human health and environmental risk. They believe that the regulatory process for the PGP has been reasonable and workable for pest control operations and agriculture interests.

In the 114ᵗʰ Congress, legislation similar to bills passed by the House in the 112ᵗʰ and 113ᵗʰ Congresses to overturn requirements for the PGP has been introduced. In the Senate, the Environment and Public Works Committee approved S. 1500 on August 5, 2015. This bill would clarify congressional intent regarding the regulation of the use of pesticides in or near U.S. waters. It differs from previous versions of the legislation in that it also would require EPA to report to Congress on better coordination of efforts by the agency's water quality and pesticides offices in order to analyze the water quality impacts of pesticides and the effectiveness of current pesticide registration actions at protecting water quality. On January 20, 2016, the Senate Environment Committee approved S. 659, the Bipartisan Sportsmen's Act of 2015, with an amendment identical to the text of S. 1500.

In the House, legislation identical to H.R. 935 from the 113ᵗʰ Congress was introduced (H.R. 897, the Reducing Regulatory Burdens Act) and was approved by the House Agriculture Committee in March 2015. The House took up this bill in May 2016 and passed a modified version on May 24, by a vote of 258-156. Proponents argued that the legislation is needed so that public health agencies that spray pesticides to respond to mosquitoes that carry the Zika virus and other diseases could focus resources on disease-carrying vectors, rather than CWA permitting. Opponents asserted that the legislation would weaken environmental protections by relaxing standards for pesticide application to the point that waterbodies will become impaired or threatened by pesticides. As passed, the legislation was re-titled the Zika Vector Control Act and modified previous versions by including a sunset provision, under which the legislation will expire on September 30, 2018, and the PGP would again become effective after that date.

Separate Senate legislation, S. 2899, the Zika Response and Regulatory Relief Act, would provide a temporary, 180-day waiver of the PGP and its reporting requirements solely for the purpose of public health pesticide applications of a mosquito control program.

Author Contact Information

Claudia Copeland
Specialist in Resources and Environmental Policy
ccopeland@crs.loc.gov, 7-7227

Zika Response Funding: Request and Congressional Action

Susan B. Epstein, Coordinator
Specialist in Foreign Policy

Sarah A. Lister
Specialist in Public Health and Epidemiology

June 2, 2016

Congressional Research Service

7-5700

www.crs.gov

R44460

Contents

Tables

Contacts

Summary

The second session of the 114th Congress is considering whether and how to provide funds to control the spread of the Zika virus throughout the Americas. Zika infection, primarily spread by *Aedes* mosquitoes, has been linked to severe birth defects and other health concerns. Local transmission of the Zika virus has occurred in American Samoa, Puerto Rico, and the U.S. Virgin Islands, and is expected on the U.S. mainland this summer, in areas where *Aedes* mosquitoes are present.

On February 22, 2016, the Obama Administration submitted a request for more than $1.89 billion in supplemental funding to respond to the Zika epidemic, all of which is requested as emergency discretionary appropriations and therefore effectively exempt from spending limits per the Budget Control Act of 2011 (BCA, P.L. 112-25). The emergency request includes $1.509 billion for the Department of Health and Human Services (HHS), $335 million for the U.S. Agency for International Development (USAID), and $41 million for the Department of State. The request also seeks authority to transfer some of those supplemental emergency appropriations across other federal agencies such as the Department of Defense, the Environmental Protection Agency, and the U.S. Department of Agriculture, to allow greater flexibility as circumstances change. It also would provide HHS, the Department of State, and USAID with broad authority for direct hiring, not be limited to positions related to Zika response efforts, and would authorize personal services contracting by HHS, State and USAID, for the Zika virus, but not limited to Zika virus efforts.

On April 6, 2016, the White House Office of Management and Budget (OMB) and the Secretary of HHS announced that they had identified $589 million—$510 million of it from "existing Ebola resources within the Department of Health and Human Services and Department of State/USAID"—that can quickly be redirected and spent on immediate efforts to control and respond to the spread of the Zika virus in the Americas.

On April 8, 2016, the Administration notified Congress of a transfer of $295 million out of the $510 million from FY2015 unobligated Ebola Economic Support Funds (ESF) to be used for the Zika response efforts. Of that amount, USAID is providing $158 million to CDC including $78 million for Zika response and $80 million for Ebola response. The remaining $137 million also from FY2015 ESF is funding various USAID activities for its Zika response efforts.

As of mid-May 2016, congressional action on supplemental appropriations for Zika-related purposes has occurred in both the House and the Senate. The Senate action occurred with regard to an amendment to the combined FY2017 Military Construction-Veterans Affairs and Transportation-Housing and Urban Development appropriations bills (S.Amdt. 3900); that amendment provides $1.1 billion, which would be available until September 30, 2017 (some until expended). House action has occurred with regard to a stand-alone supplemental appropriations bill (H.R. 5243); this bill provides $622.1 million for Zika funding, which would be available until September 30, 2016. Nearly half of the funds are designated as emergency funding. Rescissions are included. CBO scored the total budgetary effects of these rescissions as reducing budget authority by $622 million, and reducing outlays by $12 million during FY2016. On net, CBO estimates the budgetary effects of the bill to be $0 in budget authority and an increase of $9 million in outlays for FY2016.

This report will identify the various Zika response funding options and track legislation in the 114th Congress.

Introduction

In its second session, the 114th Congress is considering whether and how to provide funds to control the spread of the Zika virus throughout the Americas. Zika infection, primarily spread by *Aedes* mosquitoes, has been linked to severe birth defects and other health concerns. Local transmission of the Zika virus has occurred in American Samoa, Puerto Rico, and the U.S. Virgin Islands, and transmission is expected on the U.S. mainland this summer, in areas where *Aedes* mosquitoes are present.[1]

Federal efforts to address the outbreak include research on the infection and its effects, mosquito control measures, and efforts to develop a vaccine. The public health focus, both domestically and elsewhere in the Americas, is to protect pregnant women from infection and prevent birth defects. Administration officials and some in Congress are concerned about the resources needed to prevent widespread Zika infections as the Northern Hemisphere summer approaches.

This report presents the Administration's request for supplemental appropriations for the Zika response, supplemental appropriations measures that have received congressional action, and information about unobligated Ebola supplemental funds as of January 1, 2016 (the most recent publicly available). Updates will be forthcoming as details become available.

Administration Actions

On February 22, 2016, the Obama Administration submitted a request for more than $1.89 billion in supplemental funding to respond to the Zika epidemic, all of which is requested as emergency FY2016 discretionary appropriations, and therefore effectively exempt from spending limits in the Budget Control Act of 2011 (BCA, P.L. 112-25).[2] The Administration's request includes $1.509 billion for the Department of Health and Human Services (HHS), $335 million for the U.S. Agency for International Development (USAID), and $41 million for the Department of State. The request also seeks authority to transfer some of those supplemental emergency appropriations across other federal agencies, such as the Department of Defense, the Environmental Protection Agency, and the U.S. Department of Agriculture, to allow greater flexibility as circumstances change. It also would provide HHS, the Department of State, and USAID with two personnel management authorities for, but not limited to, addressing the Zika outbreak; broad authority for direct hiring;[3] and authority for personal services contracting.[4]

---

[1] For more information, see CRS Report R44368, *Zika Virus: Basics About the Disease*; CRS In Focus IF10353, *Mosquitoes, Zika Virus, and Transmission Ecology*; CRS Insight IN10433, *Zika Virus: Global Health Considerations*; and CRS Report R44385, *Zika Virus: CRS Experts*.

[2] White House, Office of Management and Budget, Estimate #1 – FY 2016 Emergency Supplemental: Appropriations Request to Respond to the Zika Virus both Domestically and Internationally, February 22, 2016, https://www.whitehouse.gov/omb/budget_amendments. For more information on discretionary spending limits and Ebola funds designated for emergency requirements, see OMB Final Sequestration Report to the President and Congress for Fiscal Year 2015, January 20, 2015, at https://www.whitehouse.gov/sites/default/files/omb/assets/legislative_reports/sequestration/sequestration_final_january_2015_president.pdf.

[3] For more detail, see https://www.opm.gov/blogs/Director/direct-hire-authority/.

[4] As defined in regulation, "The Government is normally required to obtain its employees by direct hire under competitive appointment or other procedures required by the civil service laws. Obtaining personal services by contract, rather than by direct hire, circumvents those laws unless Congress has specifically authorized acquisition of the services by contract." (48 C.F.R. 37.104(a)) Under this authority, federal agencies can quickly contract with individual scientists, physicians, and other experts to aid in response efforts.

A major theme in congressional debates thus far has been over whether unobligated (uncommitted for expenditure) FY2015 funds that had been provided to respond to the Ebola virus outbreak should be used to fund part of the Zika response, either temporarily or permanently.[5] On April 6, 2016, the White House Office of Management and Budget (OMB) and the Secretary of HHS announced that they had identified $589 million—$510 million of it from "existing Ebola resources within the Department of Health and Human Services and Department of State/USAID"—that could quickly be reprogrammed and spent on immediate efforts to control and respond to the spread of the Zika virus in the Americas.[6]

As part of the reprogramming, on April 8, 2016, USAID notified Congress of its intent to redirect $295 million of the $510 million from FY2015 unobligated Ebola Economic Support Funds (ESF) to be used for Zika response. Of that amount, USAID transferred $158 million to CDC, including $78 million for Zika response and $80 million for Ebola response. The remaining $137 million, also from FY2015 ESF, is to be redirected to fund various USAID activities for Zika response efforts.

Congressional Actions

On May 16, 2016, the Chairman of the House Appropriations Committee introduced the Zika Response Appropriations Act, 2016 (H.R. 5243). The bill would provide $622.1 million that would be available until September 30, 2016, for domestic and international Zika response efforts. Nearly half of the funds are designated as emergency funds. The bill also includes rescissions of certain Ebola-related appropriations and the HHS nonrecurring expenses fund.[7] Provisions in the bill provide that its appropriations shall be subject to the same requirements for funds that applied to the Consolidated Appropriations Act, 2016 (P.L. 114-113). This would include any restrictions on the use of funds that were contained therein, such as the applicable prohibitions on the use of funds for abortions. The House passed the measure on May 18, 2016, without amendment.

Senate action has occurred in the context of the FY2017 Military Construction-Veterans Affairs and Transportation-Housing and Urban Development appropriations bills. The texts of these bills were combined for the purposes of initial consideration in the Senate, and offered as a substitute amendment to an unrelated measure (S.Amdt. 3896 to H.R. 2577). On May 12, 2016, Senator McConnell (on behalf of Senator Blunt) proposed an amendment to that substitute (S.Amdt. 3900 to S.Amdt. 3896) that would provide $1.1 billion for Zika response and preparedness, which would be available until September 30, 2017 (with the exception of Global Health Funds, which would be available until expended). On May 19, 2016, the Senate adopted S.Amdt. 3900,[8] followed by the pair of appropriations measures (i.e., H.R. 2577) to which it was amended.

---

[5] Ryan McCrimmon and Jennifer Shutt, "Zika Funding Squabble Engulfs Senate, House and White House," *CQ News*, April 26, 2016.

[6] OMB, Shaun Donovan, "Taking Every Step Necessary, As Quickly As Possible, to Protect the American People from Zika," OMB blog, April 6, 2016, https://www.whitehouse.gov/omb/blog.

[7] CBO scored the total budgetary effects of these rescissions as reducing budget authority by $622 million, and reducing outlays by $12 million during FY2016. On net, CBO estimates the budgetary effects of the bill to be $0 in budget authority and an increase of $9 million in outlays for FY2016.

[8] Two other proposals for Zika-related supplemental funding were also considered as amendments to these combined appropriations bills (S.Amdt. 3898 and S.Amdt. 3899, both to S.Amdt. 3896). On May 17, the Senate voted not to invoke cloture on these amendments. No further action has occurred as of the date of this report.

See **Table 1** below for a comparison of the Administration's supplemental request, S.Amdt. 3900, and House bill H.R. 5243. For a comparison of non-monetary provisions of these measures, see **Table 2**.

Table 1. Supplemental Funding Amounts for Zika Response for FY2016: Comparison of Administration Request with Senate and House Proposals

Budget Authority in $ Millions

Agency	Administration Request	S.Amdt. 3900 as Passed in Senate	H.R. 5243 as Passed in House
CDC Subtotal	828.0	449.0a	170.0bc
HRSA: Community Health Centers for territories (non-add)	0.0	(40.0)	0.0
HRSA: National Health Service Corps for territories (non-add)	0.0d	(6.0)	0.0
HRSA: Maternal and Child Health Block Grant (non-add)	0.0d	(5.0)	0.0c
HRSA Subtotal	0.0	51.0	0.0
PHSSEF: Social Services Block Grant for territories (non-add)	0.0	(75.0)	0.0
PHSSEF: Other (non-add)	(295.0)d	(75.0)e	(103.0)
PHSSEF Subtotal	295.0	150.0	103.0
NIH/NIAID Subtotal	130.0	200.0	230.0
FDA Subtotal	10.0	0.0	0.0f
CMS Subtotal (Medicaid federal matching rate)	246.0	no provision	no provision
HHS Total	**1,509.0**	**850.0g**	**503.0**
State: Diplomatic and Consular Programs (D&CP)	14.6	14.6	9.1h
State: Emergencies in the Diplomatic and Consular Service	4.0	4.0	0.0i
State: Repatriation Loans	1.0	1.0	0.0
State: Nonproliferation, Anti-Terrorism, Demining and Related Programs (NADR)	8.0	4.0	0.0
State: International Organizations and Programs (IO&P)	13.5	13.5	0.0
USAID: Operating Expenses (OE)	10.0	10.0	10.0
USAID: Global Health Programs (GHP)	325.0	211.0	100.0i
State / USAID Total	**376.1**	**258.1**	**119.1**
REQUEST OR BILL TOTAL	**1,885.1**	**1,108.1**	**622.1**

Source: CRS analysis of text of White House, Office of Management and Budget, "Estimate #1–FY 2016 Emergency Supplemental: Appropriations Request to Respond to the Zika Virus both Domestically and Internationally," February 22, 2016, https://www.whitehouse.gov/omb/budget_amendments; S.Amdt. 3900; and H.R. 5243 IH.

Notes: Numbers in parentheses are included in subtotals.

a. Of the CDC funds provided, $88 million may be used to reimburse prior Zika response spending.

b. Of the CDC funds provided, up to $500,000 each must be transferred to the HHS Office of Inspector General and the Comptroller General for oversight activities.

c. Up to $50.0 million of the CDC funds provided may be transferred to HRSA MCH for specified activities.

d. Unspecified amounts from the PHSSEF may be transferred to HRSA for National Health Service Corps activities in the territories, and for the Maternal and Child Health Block Grant.

e. Other Public Health and Social Services Emergency Fund (PHSSEF) activities principally involve development and purchase of medical countermeasures.

f. The House-reported Agriculture and Related Agencies appropriation for FY2017 included $10 million for FDA activities related to the response to Ebola, Zika, and other emerging threats. H.Rept. 114-531, p. 70.

g. Broad authority is provided for funds to be transferred to or merged with other CDC, PHSSEF, HRSA, and NIH appropriations accounts to fund the purposes specified in the measure. Such transfers can only occur following consultation with OMB with a 10-day notification in advance, among other requirements.

h. Up to $1.35 million of funds for Diplomatic and Consular Services may be used for medical evacuation costs for any U.S. agency.

i. Up to $1.0 million of funds for Diplomatic and Consular Services may be transferred to Emergencies in the Diplomatic and Consular Service

j. Of the Global Health Program funds provided, up to $500,000 each must be transferred to the USAID Office of Inspector General and the Comptroller General for oversight activities.

Table 2. Selected Supplemental Provisions for Zika Response for FY2016: Comparison of Administration Request with Senate and House Proposals

Provision	Administration Request	Senate (S.Amdt. 3900)	House (H.R. 5243 IH)
Period of Availability of Funds			
HHS Funds	Until expended.	Until Sept. 30, 2017.	Until Sept. 30, 2016.
State / USAID Funds: D&CP: Nonproliferation, Anti-Terrorism, Demining and Related Programs; International Organizations and Programs; Operating Expenses	Until Sept. 30, 2017.	Until Sept. 30, 2017.	Until Sept. 30, 2016.
State / USAID Funds: Emergencies in the Diplomatic and Consular Service; Repatriation Loans; Global Health Programs.	Until expended.	Until expended.	Until Sept. 30, 2016.
Scope of Use of Funds			
CDC Funds	To prevent, prepare for, and respond to Zika virus, other vector-borne diseases, or other infectious diseases and related health outcomes, domestically and internationally.	To prevent, prepare for, and respond to Zika virus, other vector-borne diseases, and related health outcomes, domestically and internationally.	To prevent, prepare for, and respond to Zika virus, domestically and internationally.

Provision	Administration Request	Senate (S.Amdt. 3900)	House (H.R. 5243 IH)
HRSA Funds	(Scope for PHSSEF funds would apply to any funds transferred to HRSA.)	To prevent, prepare for, and respond to Zika virus, other vector-borne diseases, and related health outcomes, domestically and internationally.	(Scope for CDC funds would apply to any funds transferred to HRSA.)
NIH Funds	To prevent, prepare for, and respond to Zika virus, other vector-borne diseases, or other infectious diseases and related health outcomes, domestically and internationally.	To prevent, prepare for, and respond to Zika virus, other vector-borne diseases, and related health outcomes, domestically and internationally.	For development of vaccines for the Zika virus.
PHSSEF Funds	To prevent, prepare for, and respond to Zika virus, other vector-borne diseases, or other infectious diseases and related health outcomes, domestically and internationally.	To prevent, prepare for, and respond to Zika virus, other vector-borne diseases, and related health outcomes, domestically and internationally.	To respond to Zika virus, domestically and internationally.
State Dept. Diplomatic and Consular Programs (D&CP)	To support response efforts related to the Zika virus and related health outcomes, other vector-borne diseases, or other infectious diseases.	To support response efforts related to the Zika virus and related health outcomes, other vector-borne diseases, or other infectious diseases.	To support cost of medical evacuations and other response efforts related to the Zika virus and health conditions directly associated with the Zika virus.
State Dept. Emergencies in Diplomatic and Consular Service	To support response efforts related to the Zika virus and related health outcomes, other vector-borne diseases.	To support response efforts related to the Zika virus and related health outcomes, other vector-borne diseases.	No comparable provision.
Repatriation Loans Program	For direct loans to support response efforts related to the Zika virus and related health outcomes, other vector-borne diseases, or other infectious diseases.	For direct loans to support response efforts related to the Zika virus and related health outcomes, other vector-borne diseases, or other infectious diseases.	No comparable provision.
USAID Operating Expenses (OE)	To support response efforts related to the Zika virus and related health outcomes, other vector-borne diseases, or other infectious diseases.	To support response efforts related to the Zika virus and related health outcomes, other vector-borne diseases, or other infectious diseases.	Response efforts related to the Zika virus and health conditions directly associated with the Zika virus.
Global Health Programs (GHP)	For assistance or research to prevent, treat, or otherwise respond to the Zika virus and related health outcomes, other vector-borne diseases, or other infectious diseases.	For assistance or research to prevent, treat, or otherwise respond to the Zika virus and related health outcomes, other vector-borne diseases, or other infectious diseases.	For vector control activities to prevent, prepare for, and respond to the Zika virus internationally.

Provision	Administration Request	Senate (S.Amdt. 3900)	House (H.R. 5243 IH)
Dept. of State, Nonproliferation, Anti-terrorism, Demining and Related Programs (NADR)	To support response and research efforts related to the Zika virus and related health outcomes, other vector-borne diseases, or other infectious diseases.	To support response and research efforts related to the Zika virus and related health outcomes, other vector-borne diseases, or other infectious diseases.	No comparable provision.
International Organizations and Programs (IO&P)	To support response and research efforts related to the Zika virus and related health outcomes, other vector-borne diseases, or other infectious diseases.	To support response and research efforts related to the Zika virus and related health outcomes, other vector-borne diseases, or other infectious diseases.	No comparable provision.
Transfer Authority			
HHS Funds	CDC funds may be transferred within CDC. NIH funds may be transferred within NIH. PHSSEF funds may be transferred to two stated HRSA accounts, as specified, to an HHS countermeasures injury compensation fund, and to any other HHS accounts.	Any HHS funds in the amendment may be transferred to accounts in CDC, HRSA, NIH, and PHSSEF. $75 million in PHSSEF funds must be transferred to the HHS Social Services Block Grant.	CDC funds may be transferred within CDC, and to three stated HRSA accounts, as specified. NIH funds may be transferred within NIH. PHSSEF funds may be transferred to an HHS countermeasures injury compensation fund.
International Affairs	Funds may be transferred between foreign affairs accounts within the same headings to carry out the purposes of this Act and are in addition to other transfer authority within this proposal.	Funds within certain foreign affairs accounts may be transferred between foreign affairs accounts within the same headings to carry out the purposes of this Act and are in addition to other transfer authority within this proposal.	Specified funds within D&CP may be transferred for medical evacuation, transferred for Emergencies in Diplomatic and Consular Services, and are in addition to any other transfer authority within this proposal.
Notification, Reporting and Oversight			
HHS Notification Requirement for Obligation	No comparable provision.	No comparable provision.	15 days in advance of obligation.
International Affairs Notification Requirement	No comparable provision.	15 days in advance of obligation.	15 days in advance of obligation.
HHS Reporting Requirement	No comparable provision.	Within 30 days of enactment the HHS Secretary must report to the Appropriations Committees with a spend plan, followed by quarterly reports on obligations until funds have been fully expended.	Within 30 days of enactment the HHS Secretary must report to the Appropriations Committees with a spend plan, which must be updated and resubmitted every 30 days until funds have been fully expended.
International Affairs Reporting Requirement	No comparable provision.	Within 45 days after enactment and prior to obligation of international funds, the USAID	Within 30 days after enactment the Secretary of State and USAID Administrator must submit

Provision	Administration Request	Senate (S.Amdt. 3900)	House (H.R. 5243 IH)
		Administrator must submit spend plans to the Committees on Appropriations, update and resubmit to those committees every 90 days until September 30, 2017, and every 180 days thereafter until all funds are expended.	to Appropriations Committees a consolidated report and update and submitted to those committees every 30 days until all funds are expended.
HHS Oversight	No comparable provision.	No comparable provision.	$500,000 of CDC funds must be made available to the HHS Office of the Inspector General for oversight; an additional $500,000 from CDC must be made available for oversight by the Comptroller General of the United States.
International Affairs Oversight	No comparable provision.	$500,000 made available within the International Affairs Chapter is to be made available for the Comptroller General of the United States for oversight activities and for consultation with the Secretary of State and the USAID Administrator prior to obligating such funds.	$500,000 from GHP within this Title must be made available to USAID's Office of the Inspector General for oversight; an additional $500,000 from GHP must be made available for oversight by the Comptroller General of the United States.

Source: CRS analysis of text of White House, Office of Management and Budget, "Estimate #1–FY 2016 Emergency Supplemental: Appropriations Request to Respond to the Zika Virus both Domestically and Internationally," February 22, 2016, https://www.whitehouse.gov/omb/budget_amendments; S.Amdt. 3900; and H.R. 5243 IH.

The Emergency Supplemental Appropriations Request for Zika Response Efforts

The following describes the Administration's February 2016 Zika emergency supplemental request components by agency.

It was reported on April 18 that the Administration submitted a revised Zika supplemental request to Congress, which would maintain departmental request totals, while redirecting some of the HHS funds requested for contingency use to vaccine research and development at the National Institutes of Health (NIH).[9] Detailed information about this is not publicly available, and the following narrative does not reflect this revision.

---

[9] Erik Wasson, "Obama Administration Updates Zika Spending Request," *Bloomberg*, April 18, 2016.

Health and Human Services

The Administration's emergency supplemental appropriations request to respond to the Zika outbreak seeks for HHS a total of $1.509 billion. Each HHS agency request includes the statement that funds would be "to prevent, prepare for, and respond to Zika virus, other vector-borne diseases, or other infectious diseases and related health outcomes, domestically and internationally.... " Most of the requested funds would support research, surveillance, vaccine and test development, and various domestic preparedness activities. A portion would support international response activities. The request proposes that all supplemental appropriations to HHS be designated as emergency spending, and remain available until expended.

Centers for Disease Control and Prevention (CDC)

A total of $828 million of the February 2016 request is for the CDC-Wide Activities and Program Support account. Proposed request language would, among other things, authorize the CDC Director to transfer funds between CDC accounts, and authorize funds to be used for real property acquisition and improvements to non-federal facilities. Funds would be used as follows:

- **Grants and technical assistance to Puerto Rico and U.S. Territories**—$225 million to, among other purposes, monitor pregnant women and establish a registry of women infected while pregnant; expand mosquito control activities; and enhance laboratory testing capacity.

- **Domestic Response**—$453 million to provide grants to southern and other U.S. states with *Aedes* mosquitoes for surveillance, improved test methods and testing capacity, public education and outreach, mosquito control measures in areas at risk, and additional federal and state response activities.

- **International Response Activities**—$150 million to expand the public health workforce, and enhance infectious disease surveillance and emergency response activities, in Zika-affected countries; and to support the laboratory network of the Pan American Health Organization (PAHO), the regional arm of the World Health Organization (WHO) for the Americas.

Public Health and Social Services Emergency Fund (PHSSEF)

The PHSSEF is a fund used by appropriators to provide the HHS Secretary with ongoing or one-time emergency funding, such as for the response to disease epidemics. The emergency supplemental request seeks $295 million for the PHSSEF for the following:

- several maternal and child health and home visitation programs for low-income pregnant women at risk of Zika infection, and families that have children born with birth defects related to Zika infection;

- several health care workforce assistance programs for Puerto Rico and other territories; and

- compensation for persons harmed by the use of tests or vaccines used under emergency authority.[10]

---

[10] This compensation program is described in "Covered Countermeasure Process Fund" in CRS Report RS22327, *Pandemic Flu and Medical Biodefense Countermeasure Liability Limitation*, and HHS, Health Resources and Services Administration, Countermeasures Injury Compensation Program (CICP), http://www.hrsa.gov/cicp/index.html.

The requested PHSSEF funds could, in consultation with OMB, be transferred to other agencies within HHS or across the federal government. The request stated that this transfer authority is to provide flexibility in response to changing needs. No congressional notification requirement is included.

National Institutes of Health (NIH)

The emergency supplemental request seeks $130 million for the NIH National Institute of Allergy and Infectious Diseases (NIAID) to expand research efforts to characterize the progression and effects of Zika infection and other vector-borne diseases, and to develop vaccines against them.[11] Proposed request language would authorize the NIH Director to transfer funds between NIH accounts. No congressional notification requirement is included.

Food and Drug Administration (FDA)

The emergency supplemental request seeks $10 million for FDA's role in reviewing the safety and effectiveness of medical countermeasures (such as test methods, vaccines, and treatments), and post-market monitoring of such countermeasures if and when they become available.

Medicaid Funding for Territories[12]

The emergency supplemental request would temporarily increase the federal matching rate for Medicaid in the territories. The territories operate Medicaid programs under different rules from those that apply to the 50 states and the District of Columbia. Federal Medicaid funding to the states and the District of Columbia is open-ended, but the territories receive capped annual allotments (i.e., the maximum amount of federal funds available in a year). In addition, the Patient Protection and Affordable Care Act (ACA, P.L. 111-148, as amended) provides the territories with additional federal Medicaid funding to use by September 30, 2019. The territories have a federal medical assistance percentage (FMAP) rate (i.e., federal matching rate) for Medicaid of 55%.[13]

The supplemental request includes a provision that would increase the FMAP rate for the territories to 65% for one year beginning with the first day of the fiscal quarter following enactment. This increased FMAP rate would be available for all Medicaid expenditures, not limited to those provided to treat Zika infection. The federal funding for the increased FMAP rate would not count against the territories' annual federal spending caps or additional ACA funding. The Administration estimates this FMAP rate increase would cause federal Medicaid expenditures to grow by $246 million.[14]

There is some question about how this provision would affect Puerto Rico if it were to exhaust its additional ACA funding prior to FY2019.[15] Depending on the timing of enactment, Puerto Rico

---

[11] This refers to infectious diseases that are transmitted by a living organism (a "vector," such as a mosquito), from one host to another.

[12] This section contributed by Alison Mitchell, Specialist in Health Care Financing, Domestic Social Policy Division.

[13] For more information about the Medicaid program in the territories, see CRS Report R44275, *Puerto Rico and Health Care Finance: Frequently Asked Questions*, coordinated by Annie L. Mach.

[14] The funding for this provision would be provided through a change in mandatory programs (CHIMP), which is a provision in an appropriations act that affects a mandatory spending program.

[15] According to HHS, Puerto Rico is projected to exhaust its ACA Medicaid funding by the end of FY2017. HHS, *FY2017 Budget in Brief*, February, 2017, p. 97, http://www.hhs.gov/sites/default/files/fy2017-budget-in-brief.pdf.

might not have access to its full annual Medicaid allotments or additional ACA funding for a portion of the time the provision would be in effect.[16]

Retroactive Reimbursement

The request proposes language that would allow funds provided in the act to be used to reimburse HHS accounts for Zika response expenses incurred prior to enactment.

Transfer Authority

The request proposes language that would allow funds appropriated to HHS in the act to be transferred to other federal accounts, including the Department of Defense, the Environmental Protection Agency, and the Department of Agriculture "to prevent, prepare for, and respond to Zika virus, other vector-borne diseases, or other infectious diseases and related health outcomes, domestically and internationally…. ," following consultation with OMB. No congressional notification requirement is included.

Expanded Definition of "Security Countermeasure"

The request proposes language that would allow the government to support the advanced development and procurement of medical countermeasures against Zika virus through Project BioShield. Currently, Project BioShield supports only countermeasures against specific chemical, biological, radiological, and nuclear terrorist threats.[17] The proposed expansion is not limited to countermeasures against the Zika virus or vector-borne diseases, but rather is stated broadly as a "countermeasure to diagnose, mitigate, prevent, or treat harm from any infectious disease that may pose a threat to the public health."

International Assistance Programs

The Administration's February 2016 emergency supplemental appropriations request to respond to the Zika outbreak seeks for the Department of State and USAID a total of $376.1 million. This includes funds for control of the disease, prevention, surveillance, evacuating U.S. employees and American citizens, vaccine development, and diagnostic research, among other things. Specifically within the International Assistance section of the request is a request for transfer authority (without a requirement for congressional notification) with certain limitations, reimbursement authority, and hiring of personal services contractors, as well as authorization to use unobligated Ebola balances to combat Zika and other infectious diseases. Also worth noting is that, unlike HHS, funds for international assistance programs have varying periods of availability, as specified below.

---

[16] If Puerto Rico were to exhaust its ACA Medicaid funding before the end of FY2019, it would have to significantly increase its own Medicaid funding share in order to maintain the current program. This would worsen its current fiscal situation. For more information about this situation, see CRS Report R44095, *Puerto Rico's Current Fiscal Challenges*, by D. Andrew Austin.

[17] For more information, see HHS, "Project BioShield," https://www.medicalcountermeasures.gov/barda/cbrn/project-bioshield-overview/.

Department of State

A total of $41.1 million is requested for the Department of State operations, multilateral assistance within International Organizations and Programs (IO&P), and international security assistance (nuclear research and techniques) as follows:

- **Diplomatic and Consular Programs account (D&CP)**—$14.6 million to remain available until September 30, 2017. Of this amount
  - $8.4 million to support the Office of Medical Services for medical support and possible evacuation under the Chief of Mission authority of at-risk U.S. employees in Zika-affected countries; and
  - $6.2 million to support regional coordination efforts and public diplomacy outreach, among other activities.
- **Emergencies in the Diplomatic and Consular Service**—$4 million to remain available until expended to support response efforts, including potential evacuation of U.S. citizens.
- **Repatriation Loans Program**—$1 million to remain available until expended to finance repatriation loans to U.S. citizens who may seek to leave Zika-affected areas or who have been exposed to or have contracted Zika.
- **Nonproliferation, Anti-Terrorism, Demining and Related Programs (NADR)**—$8 million to remain available until September 30, 2017, for additional voluntary U.S. contributions to the International Atomic Energy Agency (IAEA), an autonomous intergovernmental organization related to the United Nations that promotes the safe, secure and peaceful use of nuclear technologies. Funds would support Zika research to develop and deploy nuclear techniques to help accelerate diagnosis, provide related specialized training, and to implement sterile insect projects to suppress mosquito populations.[18]
- **International Organizations and Programs (IO&P)**—$13.5 million to remain available until September 30, 2017, to support Zika response actions taken by UNICEF, the Food and Agriculture Organization, the WHO, and PAHO.

USAID

For the U.S. Agency for International Development, the Administration is requesting $335 million to cover USAID's health programs and implementation expenses:

- **USAID Operating Expenses (OE)**—$10 million to remain available until September 30, 2017, to support Zika response efforts.
- **Global Health Programs (GHP)**—$325 million to remain available until expended to prevent, treat, or respond to the Zika virus and related health concerns, other vector-borne diseases, or other infectious diseases. Multi-year funding commitments are requested to provide incentives for the development of global technologies such as vaccines, diagnostics equipment, and vector control innovations. Anticipated allocations include

---

[18] For more information see Aabha Dixit, IAEA Office of Public Information and Communication, "Nuclear Technique Can Help Control Disease-Transmitting Mosquitoes," February 3, 2016, https://www.iaea.org/newscenter/news/nuclear-technique-can-help-control-disease-transmitting-mosquitoes.

- $100 million to implement vector management and control activities in Zika-affected countries;
- $100 million to stimulate private sector research and development of vaccines, diagnostics, and vector control innovations through public-private partnerships;
- $50 million for maternal and child health support in affected and at-risk countries, including training of health care workers; ensuring access to family planning information, services, and methods; providing support for children with microcephaly; and helping pregnant women and their partners have access to personal protection, including condoms and repellant to protect against mosquitoes;
- $25 million for public health communication and behavior change campaigns for affected communities and countries to take actions to protect themselves from Zika and other vector-borne diseases; and
- $50 million to issue Global Health Security Grand Challenges that would call for groundbreaking innovations in diagnostics, vector control, personal protection, community engagement and surveillance, and other tools to address Zika and other infectious diseases, as well as to develop public-private partnerships to accelerate development of innovative tools and practices.

Use of Ebola Balances for Other Infectious Diseases

Within the Department of State and Other International Programs General Provisions (in addition to the General Provisions for the entire request), the supplemental request would authorize the use of unobligated Ebola Funds (Title IX, Div. J, P.L. 113-235), stating: "[Unobligated Ebola funds] shall also be available to respond to the Zika virus and related health outcomes, other vector-borne diseases, or other infectious diseases."

As of January 1, 2016, the Department of State/USAID's unobligated Ebola funds totaled nearly $1.3 billion. Of that total, about $600 million is available until September 30, 2016 (just a few months away), and about $694 million is available until expended.[9] (See the subsequent section, "HHS, State/USAID, and DOD Unobligated Ebola Response Funds.")

Transfer Authority

The Department of State and Other International Programs General Provisions in the supplemental request would allow transfer of State Department-related funds in the request only among State Department-related accounts within the request and transfer of USAID-related funds in the request only among USAID-related accounts. No congressional notification requirement is included.

Notwithstanding Authority

The supplemental's request for notwithstanding authority could allow funds from this or prior acts supporting the U.S. Zika virus response to be expended despite any previously enacted

---

[19] Based on departmental spend plans and/or quarterly reports for HHS, State/USAID, and Defense, as required by P.L. 113-235, and obtained by CRS; and additional departmental communications.

restrictions and conditions on U.S. foreign aid. For example, if enacted, this authority could allow foreign aid to be provided to states that are otherwise restricted by law: those designated as sponsors of terrorism, those with debt arrearage, human rights violators, or states that practice coercive family planning. The Department of State has indicated in the Global Health Program (GHP) section, however, that funds will provide support for "ensuring access to voluntary family planning information, services, and methods."

Direct Hiring Authority/Personal Services Contractors

The General Provisions Title in the request, and also the General Provisions Title for the Department of State and Other International Programs, allows for expedited hiring authority to directly hire staff during critical public health threats, such as Zika, and to enter into contracts with individuals who are experts in Zika-related fields. This measure does not limit direct hiring or personal services contractors only for Zika-related purposes. This authority for direct hiring and personal services contractors could be used in a broader set of public health circumstances than the Zika virus.

HHS, State/USAID, and DOD Unobligated Ebola Response Funds

In December 2014, the Consolidated and Further Continuing Appropriations Act, 2015 (P.L. 113-235), provided $5.4 billion in emergency supplemental appropriations to HHS, the Departments of State and Defense, and USAID to address the Ebola outbreak that began in West Africa in January 2014.[20] Because these funds were designated as emergency appropriations, they are effectively exempt from spending limits in the Budget Control Act of 2011 (BCA, P.L. 112-25).[21]

On April 6, 2016, the Obama Administration announced its plan to reprogram $510 million of unobligated FY2015 Ebola funding to respond to the Zika virus.[22] HHS Ebola funds may be reprogrammable without additional congressional action (subject to existing restrictions on reprogramming, including notification). This is because the relevant appropriations measures stated the funds are available for Ebola and other infectious diseases. Some have debated whether congressional action is necessary to provide the Department of State and USAID with the authority to reprogram the unobligated Ebola funds, as much of the funding was appropriated with specific language to be used to "prevent, prepare for, or respond to the Ebola disease outbreak."

Table 3 provides, by account, the original appropriated Ebola funds, remaining (unobligated) amounts, the period of funding availability, and purpose of the funds, based on quarterly reports to Congress as required by the law. As of January 1, 2016, unobligated Ebola funds totaled $2.77 billion: $1.46 billion for HHS, $1.29 billion for State/USAID, and $17.3 million for Defense. A portion of the total, $652.9 million—most of which is USAID funding—expires September 30,

---

[20] This section addresses funds provided in P.L. 113-235 only; it does not track the $88 million appropriated to HHS for Ebola-related activities in the first FY2015 continuing resolution (P.L. 113-164).

[21] For more information on discretionary spending limits and Ebola funds designated for emergency requirements, see *OMB Final Sequestration Report to the President and Congress for Fiscal Year 2015*, January 20, 2015, at https://www.whitehouse.gov/sites/default/files/omb/assets/legislative_reports/sequestration/ sequestration_final_january_2015_president.pdf.

[22] OMB, Shaun Donovan, "Taking Every Step Necessary, As Quickly As Possible, to Protect the American People from Zika," OMB blog, April 6, 2016, https://www.whitehouse.gov/omb/blog.

2016. Nearly all of the remaining unobligated funds expire September 30, 2019, or are available until expended. **Table 3** does not incorporate the Administration's announced plans to reprogram $510 million of unobligated Ebola funds.

Table 3. FY2015 Emergency Funds Appropriated for Ebola Response and Related Activities, and Unobligated Balances

Amounts are U.S. dollars in millions. Unobligated amounts are as of January 1, 2016.

Agency and Account or Activity	P.L. 113-235[a]	Unobligated Funds	Period of Availability	Purpose(s)
DEPARTMENT OF HEALTH AND HUMAN SERVICES				
CDC: International activities	603.0	369.4	Until Sept. 30, 2019	Disease control assistance to affected and neighboring countries.
CDC: Global Health Security	597.0	525.2	Until Sept. 30, 2019	Implementation of Global Health Security Agenda (GHSA) activities.[b]
CDC: Public health emergency preparedness	165.0	11.3	Until Sept. 30, 2019	Domestic preparedness and response activities, including control in health care settings, and procurement for stockpile.
CDC: State and local	255.0	56.0	Until Sept. 30, 2019	Grants to state health departments for surveillance, testing, case management.
CDC: Worker training	0.0	—	—	$10 million for this activity was transferred to NIH. See below.
CDC: Migration/quarantine	119.3	57.4	Until Sept. 30, 2019	Screening and management of entrants from affected countries/regions.
CDC: Other domestic activities	37.0	11.9	Until Sept. 30, 2019	Vaccine trials and other applied public health research.
CDC Subtotal	**1,776.3**	**1,031.2**	—	—
ASPR (PHSSEF): Hospital Preparedness Program	208.5	21.2	Until Sept. 30, 2019	Domestic training, PPE, and establishing regional Ebola Treatment Centers (ETCs).
ASPR (PHSSEF): Other prep. and response	352.2	347.4	Until Sept. 30, 2019	Not specified. Could include domestic treatment costs for affected individuals.
ASPR (PHSSEF): BARDA	157.0	3.7	Until Sept. 30, 2019	Research, development, and procurement of vaccines and treatments.
ASPR/PHSSEF Subtotal	**717.7**	**372.3**	—	—
NIH, NIAID	238.0	35.2	Until Sept. 30, 2016	Research and clinical trials on investigational vaccines and treatments.
NIH, NIAID	10.0	9.0	Until Sept. 30, 2019	Ebola responder safety training, funds transferred from CDC.
FDA	25.0	13.7	Until expended	Development, review, and regulation of vaccines and treatments.
HHS Total	**2,767.0**	**1,461.4**	—	—

Agency and Account or Activity	P.L. 113-235[a]	Unobligated Funds	Period of Availability	Purpose(s)
STATE DEPARTMENT/USAID				
USAID, Operating Expenses	19.0	15.2	Until Sept. 30, 2016	Operating costs to address Ebola outbreak in West Africa, including temporary staffing and technical support.
USAID, Inspector General	5.6	3.4	Until expended	Oversight of Ebola response in West Africa.
USAID, International Disaster Assistance (IDA)	1,436.3	542.4	Until expended	Disaster assistance to address humanitarian needs for West Africa, such as rapid response, maintaining surveillance, screening, and contact tracing.
USAID, Global Health Programs	312.0	148.0	Until expended	Expanded USAID global health security activities to control infectious diseases and limit spread of Ebola, including surveillance and building lab capacity.
State/USAID, Economic Support Fund	711.7	583.0	Until Sept. 30, 2016	Training and program assistance to prevent economic and government instability during Ebola crisis, including reimbursement for earlier response. Activities include rehabilitation of the water infrastructure, strengthening health information systems, and developing technology to prevent the spread of Ebola.
State, Diplomatic, Consular Programs (D&CP)	36.4	2.2	Until Sept. 30, 2016	Medical support and evacuation capacity, repatriation assistance, and other needs.
State, Repatriation Loans Program	ns	ns	ns	Repatriation loans to U.S. citizens as necessary related to Ebola outbreak. Funding not specified in P.L. 113-235. Explicit transfer authority is provided for up to $1 million from D&CP into this account.[c]
State, International Organizations and Programs (IO&P)	ns	ns	ns	Estimated U.S. contributions to UNMEER. Funding not specified in P.L. 113-235. Explicit transfer authority is provided for up to $35.3 million from IDA for this account.[c]
State, Contributions to International Organizations (CIO)	ns	ns	ns	Funding not specified in P.L. 113-235. Explicit transfer authority is provided for up to $35.3 million from IDA and $50 million from Global Health Programs for this account.[c]
State, Nonproliferation, Anti-terrorism, Demining, and Related Programs	5.3	0.0	Until Sept. 30, 2016	Biosafety and hazardous materials training in affected countries, efforts to mitigate illicit acquisition of Ebola virus and to promote biosecurity practices associated with outbreak response efforts.

Agency and Account or Activity	P.L. 113-235[a]	Unobligated Funds	Period of Availability	Purpose(s)
State/USAID Total	**2,526.3**	**1,294.2**	—	—
DEPARTMENT OF DEFENSE				
Defense/DARPA: Defense-wide research, development, testing, and evaluation (RDT&E)	45.0	0.8	Until Sept. 30, 2016	Developing medical countermeasures technologies (e.g., using antibodies from survivors) and shortening vaccine development time.
Defense/CBDP: RDT&E	50.0	16.4	Until Sept. 30, 2017	Research and Development, testing and evaluation.
Defense/CBDP: procurement	17.0	0.1	Until Sept. 30, 2017	Procurement of detection and diagnostic systems, mortuary supplies, and isolation transport units.[d]
Defense Total	**112.0**	**17.3**	—	—
TOTAL	**5,405.3**	**2,772.9**	—	—

Sources: Departmental spend plans and/or quarterly reports for HHS, State/USAID, and Defense, as required by P.L. 113-235, and obtained by CRS; and additional departmental communications.

Note: Amounts may not add due to rounding; "ns" means not specified.

Glossary: ASPR is HHS Assistant Secretary for Preparedness and Response; BARDA is HHS Biomedical Advanced Research and Development Authority; CBDP is Chemical Biological Defense Program; CDC is HHS Centers for Disease Control and Prevention; DARPA is Defense Advanced Research Projects Agency; FDA is HHS Food and Drug Administration; NIAID is NIH National Institute of Allergy and Infectious Diseases; NIH is HHS National Institutes of Health; PHSSEF is HHS Public Health and Social Services Emergency Fund, administered by the HHS Secretary; PPE is personal protective equipment; UNMEER is United Nations Mission for Ebola Emergency Response, and WHO is World Health Organization.

a. HHS amounts reflect transfers between the funded agencies, as permitted by the law. P.L. 113-235, 128 Stat. 2522, §604, December 16, 2014.

b. For more information, see CDC, Global Health Security Agenda, http://www.cdc.gov/globalhealth/security/index.htm.

c. P.L. 113-235, 128 Stat. 2694, §9001.

d. Explanatory statement accompanying H.R. 83, *Congressional Record*, vol. 160 (December 11, 2015), p. H9635.

Author Contact Information

Susan B. Epstein, Coordinator
Specialist in Foreign Policy
sepstein@crs.loc.gov, 7-6678

Sarah A. Lister
Specialist in Public Health and Epidemiology
slister@crs.loc.gov, 7-7320

Acknowledgments

The authors acknowledge the assistance of Frank Gottron, Specialist in Science and Technology Policy; L. Elaine Halchin, Specialist in American National Government; Don Jansen, Specialist in Defense Health Care Policy; Kate Manuel, Legislative Attorney; Alison Mitchell, Specialist in Health Care Financing;

Barbara Schwemle, Analyst in American National Government; and Jessica Tollestrup, Specialist in Social Policy, in the preparation of this report.

Panama: Political and Economic Situation and U.S. Relations

Panama's central location in the Americas (linking North and South America) and its transportation infrastructure—especially the Panama Canal, which connects the Atlantic and Pacific Oceans—make the country a global trade hub and a strategic partner for the United States. Panama has made significant political and economic progress since the December 1989 U.S. military intervention that ousted the military regime of General Manuel Antonio Noriega. The intervention was the culmination of strong U.S. pressure against the de facto political rule of Noriega, commander of the Panama Defense Forces. Since that time, the country has had six successive democratically elected civilian governments. The endurance of elected civilian democracy in Panama for more than 25 years is a significant departure from the country's previous history of military rule, including the populist rule of General Omar Torrijos (1968-1981), who initially governed as a social reformer, and the increasingly repressive rule of General Noriega (1983-1989).

Current Political Conditions

President Juan Carlos Varela was inaugurated in July 2014 to a five-year term after winning the May 2014 presidential election with 39% of the vote in a three-candidate race. President Varela hails from the center-right Panameñista Party and succeeded Ricardo Martinelli of the center-right Democratic Change party, who governed from 2009 to 2014. During his term, Martinelli was criticized at various junctures for his combative style of governing, although he remained broadly popular in large part because of the strong performance of the Panamanian economy.

Varela served as vice president under Martinelli, and he concurrently served as minister of foreign relations for two years until he was sacked by Martinelli in 2011. The break in relations involved allegations by Varela of governmental corruption. In his electoral campaign, Varela espoused anticorruption policies as a major part of his platform. During his first year, he followed through on his pledge to investigate and prosecute public corruption, including the conviction of a Supreme Court judge for falsifying documents and illegal self-enrichment.

Martinelli has been investigated over irregularities in a public welfare program; illegal wiretapping, which reportedly included targeting politicians, civil society activists, and businessmen; and illegal pardons issued at the end of his term. In December 2015, Panama's Supreme Court ordered the arrest of former president Martinelli on the illegal wiretapping charges. In May 2016, the Supreme Court asked the foreign ministry to approve an extradition request because Martinelli currently lives in United States.

Observers initially recognized President Varela for his efforts to restore credibility to the country's democratic

institutions and to combat corruption. However, the president's popularity ratings fell to 45% in May 2016 from 79% in January 2015. Observers maintain that the decline is due in part to two significant scandals. In April 2016, a group known as the International Consortium of Investigative Journalists revealed more than 11 million files of leaked confidential financial and legal records—the so-called Panama papers—from the Panamanian law firm Mossack Fonseca. These papers showed the use of Panama as an offshore tax haven by a wide range of celebrities, leaders, public officials, and even criminals worldwide. In May 2016, the U.S. Treasury Department imposed sanctions on an alleged trade-based money-laundering network associated with the prominent Waked family of Panama, which runs some 68 companies. The scandals highlight concerns regarding Panama's efforts to combat tax evasion and money laundering.

Panama at a Glance

Population: 3.93 million (2015)

Area: 75,420 sq. km., slightly smaller than South Carolina

GDP: $46.2 billion (2014, current U.S. $)

Per Capita Income: $11,130 (2014, current U.S. $)

Life Expectancy: 78 years (2015)

Leaders: President Juan Carlos Varela; Vice President and Foreign Minister Isabel de Saint Malo de Alvarado

Sources: World Bank, State Department.

Economic and Social Conditions

Panama's services-based economy has been booming since 2010, in large part because of the Panama Canal expansion and other large infrastructure projects, such as a metro system for Panama City; a third bridge over the canal (and a fourth one planned); and expansion of the country's airport, roads, and highways. Panama has one of the fastest-growing economies in the Americas. According to the International Monetary Fund, economic growth averaged almost 8% from 2010 to 2014, declined to 5.8% in 2015, and is projected to increase to 6.1% this year.

Strong economic growth and targeted social programs have contributed to poverty reduction. According to the U.N. Economic Commission for Latin America and the Caribbean, the poverty rate declined from 31% in 2005 to 21.4% in 2014, and extreme poverty fell from 14.1% to 11.5% over the same period. Nevertheless, although the World Bank classifies Panama as having an upper-middle-income economy, inequality in the country remains relatively high, with sharp regional disparities. The World Bank maintains that poverty prevails in rural areas, where extreme poverty is about 27%. In indigenous territories known as *comarcas*, extreme poverty is over 40% and lack of access to water and sanitation is common.

A recent health challenge confronting many Latin American countries, including Panama, is the Zika virus. The virus is linked to microcephaly, a severe birth defect. As of late June 2016, Panama had 283 confirmed and more than 1,000 suspected cases of Zika virus, with 5 cases of babies born with microcephaly.

Canal Expansion Project

The Panama Canal expansion, officially launched in 2007, opened on June 26, 2016. Originally, the project was to be completed in October 2014, but payment disagreements and construction problems caused delays. The project included adding a new set of locks and a new channel that will double the canal's capacity and allow it to accommodate giant container cargo ships known as post-Panamax ships.

The Panama Canal expansion is expected to reduce shipping rates between Asia and the U.S. Gulf and East coasts, resulting in savings and, over time, increased trade using that route; it is also expected to increase Latin American trade with Asia as well as intra-Latin American trade. Jorge Quijano, the Administrator of the Panama Canal Authority (ACP), which operates the canal, maintains that with the completed expansion project the canal will be able to accommodate 98% of all containerships.

Although the largest trade route using the Panama Canal is East Coast/United States to Asia, which accounted for almost 36% of all canal cargo traffic in FY2015, the second-largest trade route is East Coast/United States to West Coast/South America, which accounted for almost 16% of cargo traffic, according to ACP statistics.

Several U.S. eastern ports have been readying themselves to take advantage of the trade expansion. The ports of Baltimore, Miami, and Norfolk can now accommodate the larger ships, and dredging projects are still under way at the ports of Charleston and Savannah. A project to raise the Bayonne Bridge in New Jersey so that the Port Authority of New York and New Jersey can attract larger ships is scheduled to be completed in late 2017.

U.S.-Panamanian Relations

The United States has close relations with Panama, stemming in large part from the extensive linkages developed when the Panama Canal was under U.S. control (1914-1999) and Panama hosted major U.S. military installations. Relations have been strengthened by a bilateral free trade agreement that entered into force in October 2012 and significantly liberalized trade in goods and services, including financial services. Because Panama has a services-based economy, the country has historically run a merchandise trade deficit with the United States. In 2015, the United States ran a $7.3 billion trade surplus with Panama, exporting about $7.7 billion in goods to Panama and importing $408 million.

Panama is a key U.S. strategic partner because of its extensive transportation infrastructure, including the canal; its use of the U.S. dollar as currency; and its financial sector. However, these same characteristics make Panama vulnerable to drug trafficking, money laundering, and other organized criminal activity.

Panama is a major transit country for illicit drugs from South America because of its geographic location, large maritime industry, and containerized seaports. According to the State Department's *2016 International Narcotics Control Strategy Report*, transnational drug trafficking organizations, including Mexican and Colombian groups, use Panama's remote Darién Province (bordering Colombia) and the country's coastline and littoral zones to move illicit drugs. Drug traffickers also exploit Panama's well-developed transportation infrastructure. Money laundering in the country is believed to come in large part from the proceeds of drug trafficking. Tax evasion, financial fraud, and corruption are also believed to be major sources of illicit funds.

Panama's antidrug cooperation with the United States is strong, and, according to the State Department, the country remains one of the regional leaders in narcotics interdictions and seizures. Although Panama has improved its anti-money laundering regime, several factors have impeded the country's efforts to combat such activity, including inconsistent enforcement of laws and regulations, a judicial system susceptible to corruption and favoritism, and the existence of bearer share corporations (in which shares are owned by whoever holds the physical stock certificate and there is no record of ownership). Panama was on the multilateral Financial Action Task Force's so-called gray list of countries with deficiencies in their standards to deter money laundering and combat terrorist financing, but it was removed in February 2016.

Because Panama is relatively well developed economically compared to its Central American neighbors, the United States provides small amounts of bilateral assistance to the country. The Administration requested $3.2 million in FY2017, including $2.1 million in Foreign Military Financing to support Panama's capacity to protect its borders and maritime territory against such threats as drug trafficking. Panama, however, also receives larger amounts of assistance through the Central American Regional Security Initiative (CARSI), a U.S. regional security program begun in FY2008 to help Central American states reduce drug trafficking while advancing citizen security. Through CARSI, the United States supports programs aimed at expanding Panamanian capabilities to interdict, investigate, and prosecute illegal drug trafficking, money laundering, and other transnational crimes while strengthening the country's judicial sector.

Mark P. Sullivan, msullivan@crs.loc.gov, 7-7689

IF10430

Zika Virus in Latin America and the Caribbean: U.S. Policy Considerations

Clare Ribando Seelke, Coordinator
Specialist in Latin American Affairs

Tiaji Salaam-Blyther
Specialist in Global Health

June S. Beittel
Analyst in Latin American Affairs

June 30, 2016

Congressional Research Service
7-5700
www.crs.gov
R44545

Summary

Congress is debating how to respond to an ongoing outbreak of Zika virus, a mosquito-borne illness that has no treatment or vaccine and can cause microcephaly—a severe birth defect—and other neurological complications. As of June 16, 2016, 60 countries and territories had reported mosquito-borne transmission of the virus, 39 of which are in Latin America and the Caribbean and are reporting cases of Zika for the first time. Brazil, which has registered the most confirmed cases of Zika in Latin America, will host the summer Olympics in August 2016. Scientists expect that travel destinations in the Caribbean will see more cases as the summer's warm, rainy season continues. More than 750 U.S. citizens, including pregnant women, have become infected through either travel or sexual transmission.

Frequent business and tourist travel, combined with the close proximity and similar climates of Latin America and the southern United States, means that mosquito-borne Zika infections are likely in the United States. Zika is primarily spread by *Aedes* mosquitoes—primarily *Aedes aegypti* but also *Aedes albopictus*, the latter of which is present in a majority of U.S. states. Local (or mosquito-borne) transmission has not yet occurred in the continental United States but is occurring in Puerto Rico and the U.S. Virgin Islands.

On February 8, 2016, the Obama Administration submitted an emergency request for almost $1.9 billion in supplemental funding to respond to the Zika outbreak, including $526 million for international efforts. On April 6, 2016, the Administration announced that it would reprogram $589 million in unobligated funds, including $510 million in Ebola supplemental funds, for efforts to address the Zika outbreak. The U.S. Agency for International Development (USAID) is reprogramming $215 million of that funding—including a $78 million transfer to the U.S. Centers for Disease Control and Prevention (CDC)—for international efforts. In mid-May 2016, both the House and the Senate passed supplemental appropriations measures for Zika response. The House bill, H.R. 5243, would provide $622.1 million in Zika funding and rescind an equal amount of budget authority. The Senate measure (S.Amdt. 3900 to H.R. 2577, the combined FY2017 Military Construction-Veterans Affairs and Transportation-Housing and Urban Development appropriations bills) would provide $1.1 billion in Zika response funding without rescissions. On June 23, 2016, the House agreed to a conference agreement (see H.Rept. 114-640) that would provide $1.1 billion for Zika response, including $175.1 million for State Department and USAID activities. On June 28, 2016, the Senate voted not to invoke cloture on the conference agreement.

The number of people in the Western Hemisphere affected by Zika is unknown, but as many as 4 million people may be at risk of infection in 2016, and nearly all countries in Latin America and the Caribbean have recorded cases of the virus. Zika responses in the region have been led by Brazil and Colombia, multilateral organizations such as the World Health Organization (WHO)/Pan American Health Organization (PAHO), and the U.S. government. Health experts have expressed concerns about the capacity of health systems—particularly in Central America and the Caribbean—to prevent, diagnose, and care for Zika cases and associated complications, particularly among pregnant women. Related issues of interest to Congress include how to balance support for U.S. initiatives and multilateral approaches, the proper scope and components of U.S. health assistance to the region, and funding for pandemic preparedness and research on neglected tropical illnesses in Latin America.

This report focuses on the Latin American dimensions of the Zika virus. For more information, see CRS Report R44549, *Supplemental Appropriations for Zika Response: The FY2016 Conference Agreement in Brief*, by Susan B. Epstein and Sarah A. Lister This report will be updated periodically.

Contents

Figures

Tables

Appendixes

Contacts

Introduction

As of June 16, 2016, the World Health Organization (WHO) reported that 60 countries worldwide had experienced mosquito-borne transmission of Zika, 46 of which had never had Zika cases before (see **Figure 1**).[1] The U.S. Centers for Disease Control and Prevention (CDC) has concluded that Zika causes microcephaly (a serious birth defect involving brain damage) and is associated with Guillain-Barré syndrome (GBS, a neurological condition) and other neurological and autoimmune conditions. Latin America and the Caribbean have been most affected by this outbreak (**Figure 1**). Since February 2016, new cases in the southern parts of the region have decreased, but an increase in new cases is expected in the Caribbean during the summer months as mosquitoes hatch and bite. The United States will likely experience an increase in travel-associated cases and possibly local transmission.[2] Policymakers are concerned about the spread of Zika into the continental United States, as well as the potential that visitors traveling to the Olympics in Brazil in August could contract the virus and bring it back to their home countries.

In February 2016, WHO Director-General Margaret Chan announced that the International Health Regulations (2005) Emergency Committee on Zika virus had determined that the Zika outbreak was a Public Health Emergency of International Concern (PHEIC).[3] Shortly thereafter, President Barack Obama requested that Congress provide almost $1.9 billion in emergency appropriations to fund domestic and international responses to the outbreak. A conference agreement on Zika funding was approved by the House but remains pending in the Senate.[4] As Congress considers funding the Zika request and then exercises oversight over U.S. Zika responses in Latin America and the Caribbean, Members may consider issues such as the following:

- **Balance between U.S. bilateral and multilateral Zika responses.** Although U.S. health assistance (bilateral and regional) to Latin America in general has declined, U.S. support for the Pan American Health Organization (PAHO)[5] has increased. While considering the President's Zika request and the FY2017 budget request, Congress may discuss how much support to provide for multilateral responses in the region led by PAHO.

- **U.S. health programs in Latin America as a part of U.S. policy toward the region.** On average, roughly 10%-20% of the funds provided by the State Department and the U.S. Agency for International Development (USAID) for Latin America between FY2009 and FY2016 have been aimed at health programs. The WHO has recommended that women and men in countries with local transmission[6] of Zika be correctly informed and oriented to consider delaying pregnancy.[7] Congress may evaluate reproductive health and family planning funding in the region given the WHO recommendation and the limited access to sexual education and contraception in the region.

---

[1] WHO, *Situation Report: Zika Virus, Microcephaly, Guillain-Barré Syndrome,* June 16, 2016.

[2] Ibid.

[3] WHO, "WHO Statement on the First Meeting of the International Health Regulations (2005) Emergency Committee on Zika Virus and Observed Increase in Neurological Disorders and Neonatal Malformations," February 1, 2016.

[4] CRS Report R44460, *Zika Response Funding: Request and Congressional Action,* coordinated by Susan B. Epstein.

[5] PAHO is the WHO's regional office for the Americas.

[6] Local transmission means that mosquitoes in the area have been infected with the virus and are spreading it to people.

[7] WHO, *Prevention of Sexual Transmission of Zika Virus: Interim Guidance Update,* June 7, 2016.

Figure 1. Global Transmission of Zika: 2007-2016

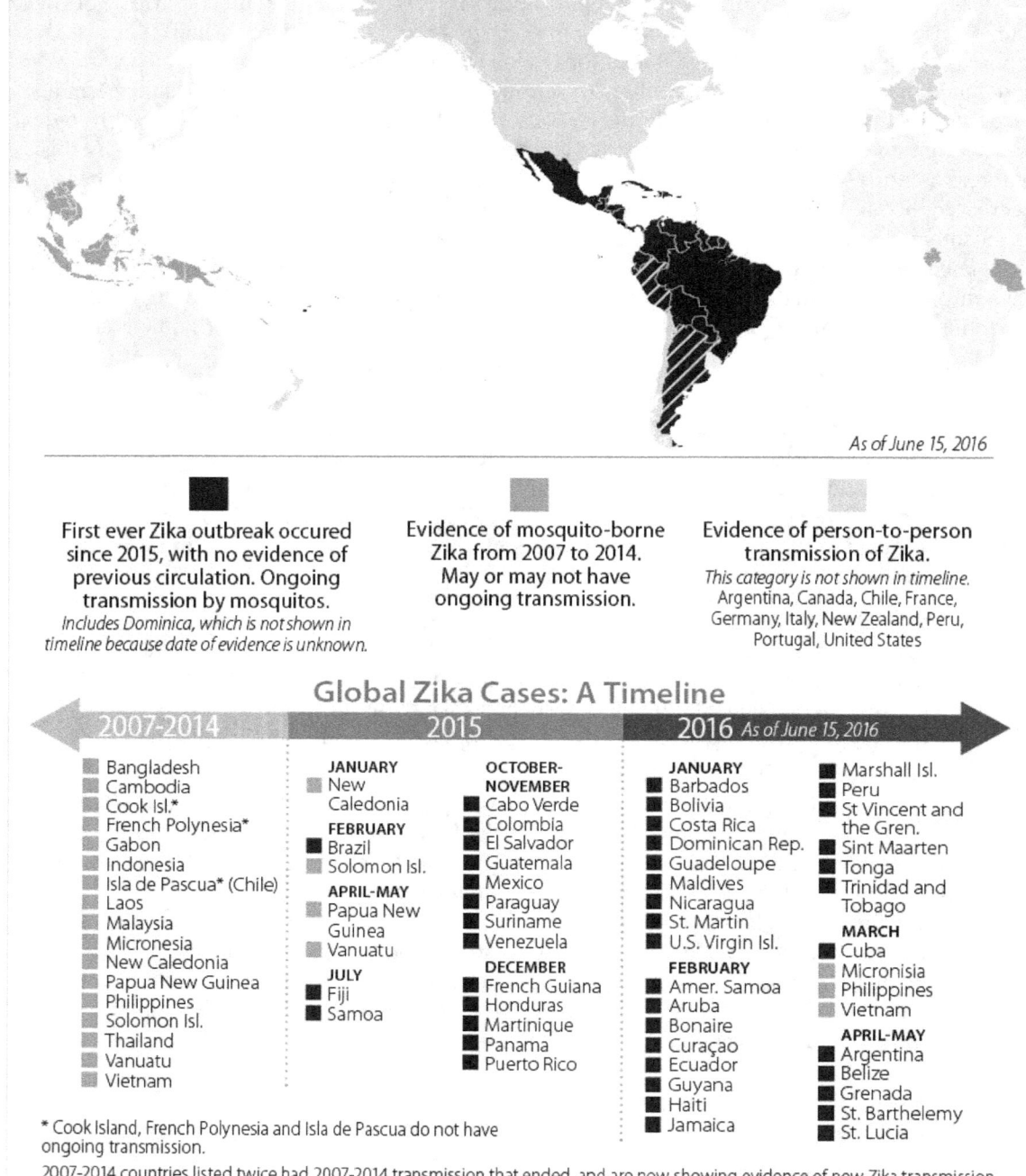

As of June 15, 2016

First ever Zika outbreak occured since 2015, with no evidence of previous circulation. Ongoing transmission by mosquitos.
Includes Dominica, which is not shown in timeline because date of evidence is unknown.

Evidence of mosquito-borne Zika from 2007 to 2014. May or may not have ongoing transmission.

Evidence of person-to-person transmission of Zika.
This category is not shown in timeline.
Argentina, Canada, Chile, France, Germany, Italy, New Zealand, Peru, Portugal, United States

Global Zika Cases: A Timeline

2007-2014 | **2015** | **2016** *As of June 15, 2016*

2007-2014
- Bangladesh
- Cambodia
- Cook Isl.*
- French Polynesia*
- Gabon
- Indonesia
- Isla de Pascua* (Chile)
- Laos
- Malaysia
- Micronesia
- New Caledonia
- Papua New Guinea
- Philippines
- Solomon Isl.
- Thailand
- Vanuatu
- Vietnam

2015

JANUARY
- New Caledonia

FEBRUARY
- Brazil
- Solomon Isl.

APRIL-MAY
- Papua New Guinea
- Vanuatu

JULY
- Fiji
- Samoa

OCTOBER-NOVEMBER
- Cabo Verde
- Colombia
- El Salvador
- Guatemala
- Mexico
- Paraguay
- Suriname
- Venezuela

DECEMBER
- French Guiana
- Honduras
- Martinique
- Panama
- Puerto Rico

2016

JANUARY
- Barbados
- Bolivia
- Costa Rica
- Dominican Rep.
- Guadeloupe
- Maldives
- Nicaragua
- St. Martin
- U.S. Virgin Isl.

FEBRUARY
- Amer. Samoa
- Aruba
- Bonaire
- Curaçao
- Ecuador
- Guyana
- Haiti
- Jamaica

- Marshall Isl.
- Peru
- St Vincent and the Gren.
- Sint Maarten
- Tonga
- Trinidad and Tobago

MARCH
- Cuba
- Micronisia
- Philippines
- Vietnam

APRIL-MAY
- Argentina
- Belize
- Grenada
- St. Barthelemy
- St. Lucia

* Cook Island, French Polynesia and Isla de Pascua do not have ongoing transmission.

2007-2014 countries listed twice had 2007-2014 transmission that ended, and are now showing evidence of new Zika transmission.

Source: Adapted by the Congressional Research Service (CRS) from World Health Organization (WHO), *Zika Virus, Microcephaly, Guillain-Barré Syndrome*, June 16, 2016.

Notes: Zika virus is not necessarily present throughout the countries/territories shaded in this map.

- **Regional apportionment and components of global health budget.** Less than 5% of all U.S. global health funds are provided to Latin America, and the majority of these funds are for HIV/AIDS programs. On average, health indicators in the region—particularly those related to maternal and child health, family planning, and reproductive health—are better than in other low- and middle-income countries, although inequities exist.[8] Congress might reexamine the apportionment of global health funding and consider whether investments in the region are sufficient to meet emerging health concerns.

- **Funding for pandemic preparedness.** The United States committed to support 30 countries (including Haiti and Peru) and the Caribbean Community (CARICOM)[9] in bolstering their ability to respond to disease outbreaks through the Global Health Security Agenda (GHSA).[10] Congress included almost $600 million in emergency Ebola appropriations to the CDC in support of GHSA and $50 million in FY2016 appropriations to USAID for pandemic preparedness activities. Congress might consider funding levels for those programs and where those funds are allotted.

- **Investments in research and development of neglected diseases.** In recent years, *Aedes* mosquitoes have caused three disease outbreaks (dengue, chikungunya, and Zika) in Latin America and the Caribbean, all of which have been imported into the United States, with the latter being only travel-associated at the time of this report. These and other diseases lack vaccines to prevent transmission, treatment regimens, and effective vector control tools. Congress might evaluate options to address threats from new and reemerging diseases, including those that are mosquito-borne.

This report provides background information on the Zika virus, discusses challenges faced by governments and implementing partners in the Latin America and Caribbean region that are attempting to control the ongoing outbreak, and analyzes the above issues in the context of the U.S. Zika response.

Background

Zika was discovered in the Zika forest of Uganda in 1947. From that time until 2007, when the first large Zika outbreak was recorded, Zika virus infection primarily caused mild symptoms (fever, skin rash, conjunctivitis, muscle and joint pain) that resolved within one week.[11] In 2007, the first large Zika outbreak was recorded on the Micronesian island of Yap. Household surveys detected 185 cases.[12]

---

[8] As an example, children from low-income families are five times as likely to die before the age of five than children from wealthier households. World Bank, "Latin America: Unequal Access to Health Care Is Still No. 1 Killer for Moms and Kids," September 11, 2013.

[9] CARICOM is a grouping of 20 countries: 15 member states and five associate members. The 15 member states are Antigua and Barbuda, Bahamas, Barbados, Belize, Dominica, Grenada, Guyana, Haiti, Jamaica, Montserrat, Saint Lucia, St. Kitts and Nevis, St. Vincent and the Grenadines, Suriname, and Trinidad and Tobago. The five associate member states include Anguilla, Bermuda, the British Virgin Islands, the Cayman Islands, and Turks and Caicos.

[10] For background on GHSA, see CRS In Focus IF10022, *The Global Health Security Agenda and International Health Regulations*, by Tiaji Salaam-Blyther.

[11] WHO, *Zika Virus*, April 15, 2016.

[12] M. K. Kindhauser et al., "Zika: The Origin and Spread of a Mosquito-Borne Virus," *Bulletin of the World Health* (continued...)

Scientists are studying the virulence of the Zika virus and the extent to which human activity affects global spread.[13] Retrospective studies of a 2013-2014 outbreak in French Polynesia linked Zika infection with GBS for the first time.[14] The current outbreak, which began in Brazil, has been accompanied with a spike in microcephaly and GBS cases, as well as other neurological and autoimmune disorders.[15] As of June 16, 2016, WHO has reported more than 1,600 cases of Zika-related microcephaly worldwide—almost all in Brazil. In addition, 13 Zika-affected countries have recorded an increased incidence of GBS.[16]

Aedes-Related Outbreaks in Latin America and the Caribbean

In the last century, Latin American and Caribbean countries have transformed from largely rural to mostly urban societies, with some 80% of all people in Latin America and the Caribbean now living in urban areas. Throughout the region, millions of people live in densely populated urban slums and poor rural communities where homes and other facilities lack air conditioning or window screens. Lack of proper plumbing and poor sanitation facilitate mosquito breeding, as mosquitoes can lay their eggs in standing water.[17] *Aedes* mosquitoes thrive in such conditions, biting during the day and breeding indoors and out.[18]

Health threats to Latin American and Caribbean populations may also be exacerbated by the 2015-2016 El Niño weather pattern, which is reflected in unusually warm water in the eastern equatorial Pacific Ocean. The present El Niño phenomenon, which has been particularly strong, has produced multiyear droughts in some areas (Colombia, Venezuela, and northern Central America) and extreme flooding in others (Argentina, Uruguay, and Paraguay). The warm, wet weather has facilitated the proliferation of mosquitoes, and human responses to drought conditions have provided favorable conditions for mosquito breeding because more people have been storing water.[19] Studies have also linked climate change with greater health threats, such as increasing prevalence of malaria, chikungunya, and dengue fever.[20] In recent years, *Aedes* mosquitoes have spread chikungunya,[21] dengue,[22] and Zika across the Americas. All three of these

---

(...continued)

Organization, February 9, 2016.

[13] Lulan Wang et al., "From Mosquitoes to Humans: Genetic Evolution of Zika Virus," *Cell Host & Microbe*, vol. 19 (May 11, 2016).

[14] Kindhauser, "Zika.". GBS is a condition in which a person's immune system attacks the peripheral nerves. Many people who develop GBS recover fully, including those with severe GBS. Severe cases of GBS are rare but can result in death. For more information on GBS, see WHO, *Guillain-Barré Syndrome*, March 14, 2016.

[15] Microcephaly is a condition in which a baby is born with a small head or the head stops growing after birth. Some babies born with mild microcephaly can live normal lives, while most babies born with severe microcephaly can experience epilepsy, cerebral palsy, learning disabilities, hearing loss, and vision problems over their lifetimes. See WHO, *Microcephaly*, March 2, 2016.

[16] WHO, *Situation Report*.

[17] According to the World Bank, at least 110 million people in Latin America lack access to modern sanitation. World Bank, "Monitoring Country Progress in Water and Sanitation," June 13, 2014.

[18] CRS In Focus IF10353, *Mosquitoes, Zika Virus, and Transmission Ecology*, by M. Lynne Corn, Tadlock Cowan, and Robert Esworthy.

[19] WHO, "El Niño May Increase Breeding Grounds for Mosquitoes Spreading Zika Virus, WHO Says," February 22, 2016.

[20] Sonia Altizer et al., "Climate Change and Infectious Diseases: From Evidence to a Predictive Framework," *Science*, vo. 341 (August 15, 2013), p. 514.

[21] Chikungunya is a virus that can cause fever and severe joint pain, which can be debilitating. Other symptoms typically include nausea, fatigue, rash, and muscle pain. There is no antiviral treatment or vaccine. From 2013 through (continued...)

---

diseases have been imported into the United States and can become locally transmissible because the *Aedes* mosquito resides in large segments of the United States.

Figure 2. Estimated Range of *Aedes* Mosquito in the United States

Aedes aegypti   Aedes albopictus

Source: CDC, "Estimated Range of *Aedes aegypti* and *Aedes albopictus* in the United States, 2016 Maps," http://www.cdc.gov/zika/vector/range.html, accessed on May 23, 2016.

Notes: Maps represent an estimate of the potential range of the *Aedes* mosquito. They are not intended to represent risk for spread of Zika.

Zika in Latin America and the Caribbean

Scientists are unsure how many people have been infected by Zika in the Western Hemisphere, but as many as 4 million people may be at risk of infection, and nearly all countries have recorded cases.[23] As of June 16, 2016, Brazil had 159,914 suspected Zika cases, almost 40,000 of which have been confirmed through diagnostic testing (see **Figure 3**).[24] Since the outbreak began in

---

(...continued)

2015, more than 1.7 million people contracted the disease, and 258 people died. During that time period, CDC estimated that 3,113 cases were imported into the United States and 11 cases were contracted locally in Florida. From the beginning of 2016 through June 17, 2016, PAHO/WHO reported 130,138 chikungunya cases in the region, of which 18,220 have been confirmed. On May 31, 2016, the Texas Department of State Health Services reported the first locally acquired chikungunya case, indicating that mosquitoes within the United States now carry the virus. WHO, "Fact Sheet: Chikungunya," April 2016; U.S. Department of Defense, *Chikungunya in the Americas Surveillance Summary #49*, September 9, 2015; WHO/PAHO, *Number of Reported Cases of Chikungunya Fever in the Americas, by Country or Territory 2016*, June 17, 2016; Texas Department of State Health Service, "DSHS Announces First Texas Acquired Chikungunya Case," press release, May 31, 2016.

[22] Dengue is a virus that can cause severe, flu-like symptoms and can cause death in about 1%-2% of all cases. Severe dengue is evidenced by severe abdominal pain, repeated vomiting, rapid breathing, bleeding gums, or blood in vomit. It is a leading cause of death for children in some Latin American countries. There is no specific treatment for dengue, but a vaccine was introduced in a few countries in late 2015. From the beginning of 2014 through June 17, 2016, PAHO estimated that more than 5 million people had contracted dengue in the region and more than 2,500 people died of the disease. Some 1,299 of these cases occurred in the United States, and no deaths were reported. WHO, "Fact Sheet: Dengue and Severe Dengue," April 2016 and WHO/PAHO, *Number of Reported Cases of Chikungunya Fever in the Americas*.

[23] Greg Botelho, "Zika Virus 'Spreading Explosively,' WHO Leader Says," CNN, February 20, 2016.

[24] PAHO/WHO, *Cumulative Zika Suspected and Confirmed Cases Reported by Countries and Territories in the Americas, 2015-2016*, June 16, 2016.

Colombia, the country had recorded 82,935 suspected cases, more than 8,000 of which have been confirmed.[25] Two key factors complicate efforts to count Zika cases:

1. About 75% of infected people do not develop symptoms.
2. The virus is detectable for less than seven days in infected people's blood.[26]

Zika: From Latin America to the United States and U.S. Territories

As of June 16, 2016, all Zika cases detected in the continental United States[27] (755) had been either acquired abroad or sexually transmitted, although the U.S. Virgin Islands, American Samoa, and Puerto Rico have experienced local transmission by mosquito. CDC and other health experts are preparing for the likelihood that the continental United States may experience locally acquired Zika cases this summer.[28] Given the broad range of the *Aedes* mosquitoes (see **Figure 2**) and the fact that mosquito-borne diseases have been imported into the United States previously, a successful response to the Zika outbreak may require U.S.-Latin American cooperation in surveillance, research, and response over several years.

The Zika Virus Outbreak in the U.S. Territories[29]

Although Puerto Rico and the U.S. Virgin Islands are U.S. territories, when it comes to the Zika virus, their locations, climate, and ecology put them in company with much of Latin America and the Caribbean. PAHO is tracking the spread of the Zika virus in Puerto Rico, the U.S. Virgin Islands, and countries across Latin America and the Caribbean. On June 2, 2016, PAHO commented, "A downward trend of cases of Zika virus disease in Central and South America continues to occur while in most Caribbean countries and territories the trend continues to rise."

As of June 15, 2016, none of the 50 U.S. states had identified local transmission of Zika virus. However, local transmission was first identified in Puerto Rico in December 2015 and in the U.S. Virgin Islands in January 2016. Puerto Rico has now identified more than 1,300 laboratory-confirmed cases, including more than 140 pregnant women. Puerto Rico is working with the CDC to actively monitor these women and assure that they and their babies receive the best possible pre- and post-natal care. Full-term babies from the earliest of these pregnancies will be due in mid- to late summer. More than 20 locally acquired cases of the Zika virus have been identified in the U.S. Virgin Islands. Puerto Rico's Zika outbreak comes amid a fiscal emergency in the territory. The Obama Administration has requested assistance for Puerto Rico and the other territories as part of emergency supplemental appropriations for the national and global response to the Zika outbreak. Congress is considering an appropriations package at this time.

Sources and additional information: CRS Report R44460, *Zika Response Funding: Request and Congressional Action*; CRS Report R44275, *Puerto Rico and Health Care Finance: Frequently Asked Questions*; CRS Report R44095, *Puerto Rico's Current Fiscal Challenges*; CDC, "Zika Virus," http://www.cdc.gov/zika/; PAHO, "Zika Virus Infection," http://www.paho.org/zika.

---

[25] Ibid.

[26] CDC, "Interim Guidance for Zika Virus Testing of Urine—United States, 2016," *Morbidity and Mortality Weekly Report*, vol. 65, no. 18 (May 13, 2016).

[27] CDC, "Zika Virus Disease in the United States, 2015-2016," http://www.cdc.gov/zika/geo/united-states html (accessed on June 16, 2016).

[28] Dan Diamond, "Frieden: CDC Will Lose Zika Fight Without Funding," *Político*, May 26, 2016.

[29] This text box was authored by Sarah A. Lister, Specialist in Public Health and Epidemiology.

Figure 3. Confirmed and Suspected Zika Cases by Country

(as of June 16, 2016)

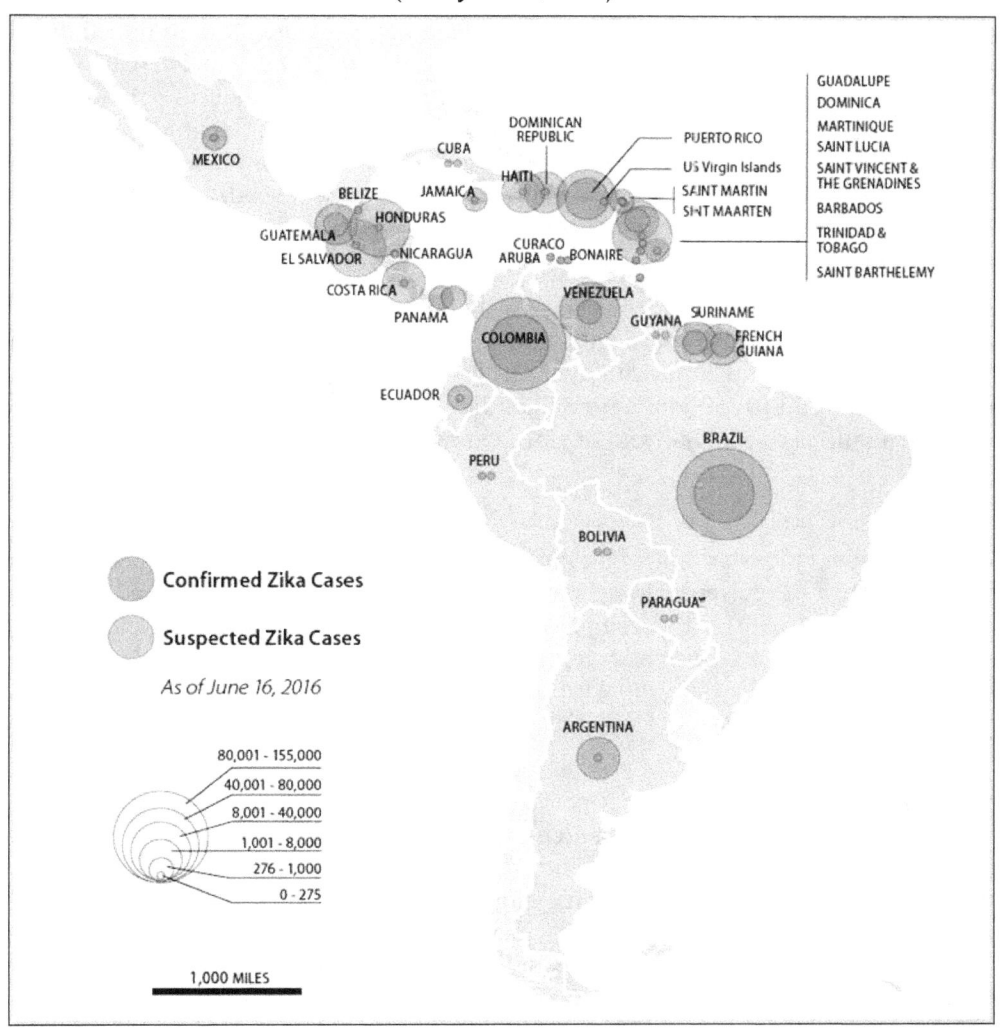

Source: Adapted by WHO/PAHO, *Cumulative Zika Suspected and Confirmed Cases Reported by Countries and Territories in the Americas,* June 17, 2016.

International Zika Responses in Latin America and the Caribbean

Country Efforts

The number of Zika cases, the capacity of health systems to address them and related complications, and the plans to do so vary widely across Latin America and the Caribbean. Haiti, for example, lacks a functioning hospital system, and Venezuela has little capacity to provide basic maternal and child health care at this time. In terms of preparedness and response to epidemiological emergencies, including Zika, recent assessments of core capacities under the International Health Regulations carried out by PAHO have highlighted weaknesses in health system capacity in all Caribbean countries (including Suriname and Guyana), selected countries of Central America (El Salvador, Guatemala, Honduras, and Nicaragua), Bolivia, and Paraguay. The Inter-American Development Bank (IDB) shares this view.[30]

Experts are concerned that these countries and several others are much less equipped than Brazil and Colombia—two of the six countries in the Americas that PAHO deemed capable of handling a pandemic illness in 2012—to address Zika and related health consequences.[31] Inadequate laboratory and diagnostic capacity, poor access to sexual education and contraception, and resistance to national mosquito control efforts due to mistrust of government authorities have hindered efforts in some countries. Gang violence and insecurity have also reportedly prevented health workers from providing services in some parts of El Salvador and Honduras.

Should Zika-associated cases of microcephaly become more common outside of Brazil, the health systems in the region may come under strain. Most countries in Latin America and the Caribbean lack the capacity to treat children born with severe birth defects and do not generally permit abortion.[32] Lifetime care for a child with microcephaly can be expensive. In the United States, such care can cost up to $10 million.[33] Brazil has struggled to care for infants with microcephaly, many of whose families live hours from one of the few hospitals that can provide care.

Brazil[34]

Brazil has been at the epicenter of the ongoing Zika outbreak, with 159,914 suspected Zika cases since the beginning of the current outbreak, of which 39,993 have been confirmed as of June 16, 2016.[35] On November 11, 2015, Brazil's Ministry of Health declared a Public Health Emergency of National Importance in response to a sharp increase in the number of infants born with microcephaly. Whereas fewer than 200 cases of microcephaly were reported annually in Brazil prior to 2015, Brazil's Ministry of Health detected 1,581 microcephaly cases between the start of 2015 and June 16, 2016.[36]

In Brazil, as in most countries in Latin America, a diagnosis of microcephaly in utero does not meet the government's standards under which abortion is permissible.[37] As a result, Brazil's Ministry of Health has issued guidelines for providing physical and occupational therapy to children born with microcephaly and is certifying hospitals capable of providing care to those infants. Brazil's congress passed a law to provide a small monthly stipend to families caring for microcephalic children, many of whom are led by single mothers who have lost the ability to maintain employment due to the type of care microcephalic babies require. Many observers are concerned that there may be a rise in illegal abortions (and possibly maternal mortality due to unsafe abortions) in Brazil as a result of increasing diagnoses of microcephaly.[38]

---

[30] CRS correspondence with health experts at the Inter-American Development Bank, June 22, 2016.

[31] PAHO, *Strategic Plan of the Pan-American Health Organization: 2014-2019,* September 2013. As of 2012, PAHO deemed six countries—Brazil, Canada, Chile, Colombia, Costa Rica, and the United States—capable of addressing pandemic outbreaks.

[32] Guttmacher Institute, "Fact Sheet: Abortion Laws in Latin America and the Caribbean," May 2016.

[33] National Public Radio, "CDC Waits for Congress to Approve Emergency Funds to Combat Zika," May 17, 2016.

[34] Peter J. Meyer, Analyst in Latin American Affairs, contributed to this section. For more on Brazil, see CRS Report RL33456, *Brazil: Background and U.S. Relations*, by Peter J. Meyer.

[35] WHO, *Situation Report.*

[36] Ibid.

[37] Marcia Castro, "Zika Virus and Health Systems in Brazil: From Unknown to a Menace," *Health Systems & Reform,* May 3, 2016.

[38] Brent McDonald, "Brazil's Abortion Restrictions Compound Challenge of Zika Virus," *New York Times,* May 18, (continued...)

The Brazilian government has launched a National Plan to Combat the *Aedes* Mosquito and Microcephaly, which includes research, prevention, and mosquito control efforts, as well as health assistance for pregnant women and children. Brazil has several world-class research institutions with vast experience in tropical diseases, and the country's national public health institutions are working with local and international partners to develop more efficient diagnostic kits, antiviral drugs, and a Zika vaccine.[39] The government has dispatched 220,000 troops and 300,000 health agents to communities around the country to educate the population and eliminate mosquito breeding grounds. Officials have placed particular focus on mosquito-control efforts in Rio de Janeiro, which is scheduled to host the 2016 Summer Olympic Games in August.

2016 Summer Olympics in Rio de Janeiro, Brazil, and the Zika Outbreak

Ongoing debate concerns whether the arrival of hundreds of thousands of tourists to Rio de Janeiro, Brazil, in August for the summer Olympics will hasten the global spread of the Zika virus. For some time, Brazilian officials have sought to assuage the fears of athletes and fans by pointing out that the Olympics will be occurring during the dry, winter season in Brazil, when fewer mosquitoes are present, and that all the venues and hotel areas will be regularly fumigated in preparation for the games. Regardless of those assurances, some health officials have called for the Olympics to be postponed or called off entirely. They have expressed concern that the strain of Zika present in Brazil, which has been linked to microcephaly and neurological problems, has been exported to Cape Verde, Africa. In May 2016, 150 health experts and bioethicists wrote an open letter to the WHO director-general urging her to recommend postponing the Olympics. In addition, some widely known athletes have indicated that they will skip the Rio Olympics due to concerns about the Zika virus.

Others oppose the proposal, noting that nonpregnant travelers going to Brazil can take sensible precautions to avoid mosquito bites and, upon returning home, use mosquito repellant (to avoid infecting mosquitoes) and use condoms to prevent sexual transmission of Zika. WHO made earlier statements indicating that "cancelling or changing the location of the 2016 Olympics will not significantly alter the international spread of Zika virus." On June 14, 2016, the WHO Emergency Committee on Zika met and reaffirmed its decision that "there is a very low risk of further international spread of Zika virus as a result of the Olympic and Paralympic Games as Brazil will be hosting the Games during the Brazilian winter when the intensity of [local] transmission of arboviruses, such as dengue and Zika viruses, will be minimal." U.S. epidemiologists calculated that the Olympic visitors would account for only 0.25% (i.e., less than 1%) of the total risk for spreading Zika through air travel.

Sources: Lena H. Sun, "150 Experts Say Olympics Must Be Moved or Postponed Because of Zika," *Washington Post*, May 27, 2016; WHO, "WHO Statement on the Third Meeting of the International Health Regulations (2005) (IHR(2005)) Emergency Committee on Zika Virus and Observed Increase in Neurological Disorders and Neonatal Malformations," June 14, 2016; Reuters, "New Research Finds Low Risk of Zika Virus at Olympics,' June 7, 2016.

Some observers have expressed concerns about the adequacy of Brazil's efforts, particularly in low-income areas. Although Brazil has one of the most advanced public health systems in Latin America, significant discrepancies exist in the quality of prenatal care and child mortality rates between the poor north and northeast regions, where many Afro-descendants live (and many Zika cases have been concentrated), and the wealthier south.[40] Reports also indicate that many states in Brazil's northeast region ran out of mosquito larvicide last year and that the country's fiscal challenges and political instability have inhibited some Zika responses this year.[41]

(...continued)

2016.

[39] Luiz Alberto Figueiredo Machado, "Brazil Is Doing Its Part in the Global Fight Against Zika," *Americas Quarterly*, February 4, 2016.

[40] Kwame A. Nyarko et al., "Explaining Racial Disparities in Infant Health in Brazil," *American Journal of Public Health*, 2013, p. 103; Olga Khazan, "What the U.S. Can Learn from Brazil's Healthcare Mess," *The Atlantic*, May 8, 2014.

[41] Castro, 2016; Stephen Eisenhammer and Pedro Fonseca, "Brazil Health Service Cracking Under Strain of Microcephaly," Reuters, February 23, 2016.

Colombia

Colombia has the second-most cases of reported Zika virus infection in the Western Hemisphere. As of June 16, 2016, Colombia had reported 82,935 suspected cases, roughly 8,000 of which have been confirmed.[42] Two-thirds of Colombia's municipalities have reported suspected or confirmed cases, and Colombia's National Institute of Health estimates that between 200,000 and 300,000 people may contract the disease in the country by the end of 2016.[43]

Similar to Brazil, Colombia has a relatively sophisticated public health system. Over the past several years, Colombia has spent a little over $15 million annually on combating contagious pathogens. It plans to maintain that funding level in 2016.[44] The Colombian Ministry of Health issued a Zika virus risk-based preparedness and response plan in January 2016 that included four key elements:

1. Strengthening the national system of epidemiological surveillance;
2. Training health personnel on early detection, diagnosis, and management of Zika cases;
3. Coordinating Zika awareness, prevention, and response activities; and
4. Bolstering health care services to improve capacity to address Zika cases and related illnesses and to implement guidelines for comprehensive care of patients.

In January 2016, the Colombian Minister of Health visited the main cities around the country to raise awareness about Zika and build support for countering the disease among local health officials. The Ministry of Health also released policy recommendations that advised couples in affected areas to use contraceptive methods to prevent possible sexual transmission of the virus and postpone pregnancy. The government allotted an additional $1.4 million to purchase necessary supplies and improve institutional support to prevent and combat Zika.

As of June 16, 2016, Colombia had seven confirmed cases of microcephaly.[45] Some experts predict that Colombia may see an increase in microcephaly cases in the coming months because its Zika outbreak began roughly six months after Brazil's. Others maintain that numbers may not grow significantly because abortion is legal under certain circumstances in the country, and some pregnant women may opt to abort after a prenatal microcephaly diagnosis.[46] Colombian officials predict that about 300 Zika-linked microcephaly cases may be diagnosed between May and September 2016.[47] The government is working with the U.S. CDC to monitor and treat women infected with the Zika virus.

---

[42] WHO/PAHO, *Cumulative Zika Suspected and Confirmed Cases*.

[43] CRS communication with the Ministry of Health in Colombia, May 23, 2016.

[44] Ibid.

[45] WHO, *Situation Report*.

[46] Colombian law reportedly allows abortions for pregnancies resulting in "malformations incompatible with life," as well as those that pose a "risk the physical, mental, or social health" of a woman. See Justin Calderon, "Colombia's Pro-Lifers Are Objectively Pro-Zika," *Foreign Policy*, April 18, 2015.

[47] CRS communication with the CDC on May 19, 2016; *El Colombiano*, "En Colombia Hay Cinco Casos Confirmados de Microcefalia por Zika," May 21, 2016.

Multilateral Organizations

WHO and PAHO

In 2015, Brazil experienced an unusual spike in microcephaly cases. Evidence later emerged linking Zika with microcephaly. The phenomenon prompted WHO Director-General Margaret Chan to convene an emergency committee on Zika virus to discuss four key issues:

5. The association of Zika infection with birth malformations and neurological syndromes;

6. The potential for further international spread of the virus given the wide geographical distribution of the mosquito vector;

7. The lack of population immunity in newly affected areas; and

8. The absence of vaccines, specific treatments, and rapid diagnostic tests.[48]

Upon recommendations of the emergency committee, Chan declared that the Zika outbreak was a PHEIC in February 2016. A PHEIC declaration signals that the health event may require immediate international action and often prompts a coordinated, multinational response. Also in February, the WHO released an interim Strategic Response Framework and Joint Operations Plan to guide the international response to the outbreak and related complications from January 2016 to June 2016. The plan focused on the following:

- Strengthening disease surveillance,

- Building laboratory capacity to detect the virus,

- Bolstering mosquito control,

- Providing care for infected persons, and

- Defining and supporting priority research areas.[49]

The plan asked for donors to provide $25 million to WHO (to coordinate and support global responses to the outbreak and scientific studies on the virus) and PAHO (to coordinate and support implementation of responses in the Americas). The remaining $31 million in funds was requested for partner organizations, including the U.N. Children's Fund (UNICEF) and U.N. Population Fund.[50]

Due to sluggish contributions, in May 2016, U.N. Secretary General Ban Ki-moon announced the establishment of a U.N. Zika Response Multi-Partner Trust Fund to attract support for unfunded priorities outlined in the aforementioned WHO strategic framework. As of June 22, 2016, donors had provided more than $4 million (16%) to the WHO/PAHO portion of the request.[51] In addition, WHO released $3.8 million in emergency support for the Zika response. WHO and PAHO do not count the emergency funds toward fundraising goals, as these funds are to be reimbursed.

---

[48] WHO, "WHO to Convene an International Health Regulations Emergency Committee on Zika Virus and Observed Increase in Neurological Disorders and Neonatal Malformations," January 28, 2016.

[49] WHO, *Zika Virus Outbreak Global Response: Interim Report*, May 27, 2016.

[50] UNICEF is working with governments and local communities to prevent the spread of Zika by eliminating mosquito breeding sites and distributing insect repellant and bed nets. UNICEF is also providing support for the care of infants born with microcephaly. The U.N. Population Fund is helping women of childbearing age in Zika-affected countries access information about Zika in pregnancy, contraception (to reduce the risk of contracting Zika while pregnant), and counseling services.

[51] WHO, *Zika: Response Funding*, June 22, 2016, http://who.int/emergencies/zika-virus/response/contribution/en.

On June 16, 2016, WHO issued a revised $122 million Zika Strategic Response Plan to guide international efforts from July 2016 through December 2017.[52] The plan describes how the WHO/PAHO and 60 partner organizations aim to bolster detection, prevention, care and support, and research on Zika and related complications. It prioritizes support for women of childbearing age and their partners in communities affected by Zika. In addition, the plan urges countries and donors to bolster investments in counseling, reproductive health services, abortions (where legal), and postnatal follow-up and care for women who have been infected with Zika and for children born with microcephaly. It also calls for expanding services and research on GBS.

Since 2015, PAHO has been working with the U.S. CDC, USAID, National Institutes of Health (NIH), U.S. Department of Defense (DOD), and other leading research entities in the region to fill in significant knowledge gaps about Zika, its transmission, and its complications and to develop new diagnostic tests and hasten progress toward creating a vaccine. PAHO has partnered with governments, U.N. entities, multilateral development banks, and private organizations on disease surveillance, mosquito abatement, community engagement and education campaigns on personal protection, and services for those affected. PAHO, the World Bank, and the IDB have developed an assessment tool that measures country capacity to handle anticipated Zika cases and accompanying complications.[53]

World Bank

In recent years, the World Bank has scaled back many of its health programs in Latin America to focus on regions with greater health needs, particularly sub-Saharan Africa. Nevertheless, the World Bank has maintained health strengthening projects in Argentina, Brazil, Nicaragua, and El Salvador and is launching a new project in Panama.[54] It is also analyzing countries to forecast the impact of major events, such as Zika, on economies in affected countries. In February 2016, the World Bank initially estimated that the costs of the Zika outbreak to Latin America would be moderate at $3.5 billion, or roughly 0.06% of regional gross domestic product.[55] Officials have since stated, however, that the impact could be greater, particularly for Caribbean countries dependent on tourism from non-Zika affected countries.[56]

Since the Zika outbreak began in Latin America, the World Bank has made $150 million available for assistance. Most of the funding would be made available by restructuring existing projects to include components focused on Zika or by including Zika-related activities in new projects. Nine countries in Latin America qualify for International Development Association[57] aid based on their low per-capita incomes. These countries can therefore access a "crisis response" window that would provide new money (including grants or credits). As of mid-June 2016, Guyana had asked for $5 million from the crisis response window.[58] El Salvador had allocated $4 million from an

---

[52] WHO, *Zika: Strategic Response Plan*, June 2016.

[53] Those dimensions include the country's capacity to (1) conduct surveillance of the disease, (2) diagnose cases, (3) launch an emergency response, (4) coordinate among various ministries, (5) conduct research, (6) monitor and report on arboviruses, (7) monitor and control complications related to Zika, (8) manage costs, and (9) provide needed health services.

[54] CRS phone interview with World Bank officials, May 12, 2016.

[55] World Bank, *The Short-Term Costs of Zika on Latin America and the Caribbean*, February 18, 2016.

[56] Center for Strategic and International Studies (CSIS), "2016 Global Development Forum: Combating Infectious Disease: The Unfolding Threat of Zika," May 19, 2016.

[57] The International Development Assistance countries are Bolivia, Dominica, St. Vincent, Grenada, Guyana, Haiti, Honduras, St. Lucia, and Nicaragua.

[58] Information in the remainder of this section is from CRS communication with World Bank officials, June 16, 2016.

existing health project, and Nicaragua had allocated $1 million from an existing project for Zika responses. Two states in Brazil had requested $20 million. Another large effort with the federal government of Brazil to address Zika had been put on hold due to the political challenges unfolding in the country.

Inter-American Development Bank

The IDB has an active portfolio of loans and grants for health programs in Latin America totaling roughly $2.7 billion. The largest programs are in Brazil, Mexico, the Dominican Republic, El Salvador, Nicaragua, and Panama. Most IDB programs focus on health system strengthening to enable governments to improve the provision of maternal and child health care and to better address noncommunicable diseases. The IDB is considering a request from the Caribbean Health Agency and a joint proposal from four South American countries to help improve those countries' compliance with International Health Regulations (2005)[59] and assist in planning for health emergencies.

In response to the Zika outbreak, the IDB has offered to reorient up to $180 million of its current portfolio of water, sanitation, and health programs to address Zika.[60] Of the $60 million in health financing made available, the IDB had received requests to reorient $19 million as of mid-May 2016. IDB efforts to address Zika are generally focused on providing family planning in rural areas using community health workers, training primary care workers to detect nervous-system problems, and distributing supplies to prevent mosquito bites. The IDB is also supporting communications campaigns and efforts to increase surveillance capacity and vector control. In addition, the IDB has collaborated with New York University to launch a crowdsourcing project that would enable governments to seek and partner with global health experts for responses to Zika and other infectious disease outbreaks.

U.S. Government

Supplemental Request

In February 2016, President Barack Obama requested almost $1.9 billion in emergency supplemental funding to address the Zika outbreak (**Table A-1**), the bulk of which was requested for the Department of Health and Human Services (HHS) primarily for domestic responses. The Administration requested that $376 million of those funds be used by USAID and the Department of State for international responses and $150 million be used for CDC international responses.

Reprogrammed Funds for USAID and CDC Programs

On April 6, 2016, the Administration announced that it would reprogram $589 million in unspent Ebola funds to address the Zika outbreak. USAID is reprogramming $215 million of that funding to support short-term efforts in Latin America, including a transfer of $78 million to CDC for

---

[59] The International Health Regulations (2005) requires WHO Member States to (1) notify WHO of any event that may constitute a PHEIC and respond to requests for verification of information regarding such events, (2) follow WHO recommendations concerning appropriate public health responses to the relevant PHEIC, (3) build and maintain core public health capacities for disease surveillance and response, and (4) collaborate with other member states to provide or facilitate the delivery of technical assistance in support of developing and maintaining core public health capacities among all member states. See CRS In Focus IF10022, *The Global Health Security Agenda and International Health Regulations*, by Tiaji Salaam-Blyther.

[60] CRS correspondence with IDB, May 17, 2016.

Zika activities in the region and a $4 million transfer to the Department of State for a contribution to the International Atomic Energy Agency. The largest components of USAID funds are to support vector control programs ($50 million) and to fund a grand challenge to encourage innovative responses to vector control, diagnostics, surveillance, and personal protection ($30 million). By far the largest component of USAID's transfer to CDC is to support surveillance, epidemiology, and public health studies ($44 million). (See **Table A-2**.)

USAID and CDC are determining where to program their activities based on the anticipated numbers of cases in each country (based on experience with dengue and chikungunya) and the anticipated needs of countries in the region. Central America and the Caribbean are top priorities. Unlike the supplemental request, which included $10 million for operating costs, the reprogrammed funds will be implemented with existing staff and resources (although USAID may use program funding to hire some staff).[61] The funds are expected to last for a year at most.[62]

Congressional Action on the Budget Request[63]

In mid-May 2016, both the House and the Senate passed supplemental appropriations measures for Zika response. The House bill, H.R. 5243, would provide $622.1 million in Zika funding and rescind an equal amount of budget authority. The Senate measure (S.Amdt. 3900 to H.R. 2577, the combined FY2017 Military Construction-Veterans Affairs and Transportation-Housing and Urban Development appropriations bills) would provide $1.1 billion in Zika response funding without rescissions. On June 23, 2016, the House agreed to a conference agreement (see H.Rept. 114-640) that would provide $1.1 billion for Zika response, including $175.1 million for State Department and USAID activities. On June 28, 2016, the Senate voted not to invoke cloture on the conference agreement.

Issues to Consider

Congress is considering a range of domestic and international responses to the Zika outbreak. In the global context, as summarized above (see "Congressional Action on the Budget Request"), Members are debating the appropriate response to the outbreak.[64] In the international context, Congress may consider how to balance support for U.S. bilateral and multilateral Zika responses. U.S. foreign assistance to Latin America and the Caribbean has been declining since FY2011, and USAID has been phasing out many global health programs in the region. The Zika outbreak may prompt broader discussions about whether to bolster U.S. global health investments in the Western Hemisphere, including in reproductive health. Discussions about controlling the Zika outbreak may also focus on U.S. support for global pandemic preparedness efforts, as well as research and development for diagnostics, treatments, and prevention measures for certain neglected diseases.

---

[61] CRS correspondence with USAID, June 22, 2016.

[62] CRS interview with USAID personnel, May 3, 2016.

[63] This section draws from CRS Report R44549, *Supplemental Appropriations for Zika Response: The FY2016 Conference Agreement in Brief*, by Susan B. Epstein and Sarah A. Lister.

[64] Ibid.

Balancing Support for Multilateral and Bilateral Zika Responses

The bulk of U.S. bilateral and regional health assistance for Latin America and the Caribbean is provided by the State Department and USAID. Since the start of the Obama Administration, State Department and USAID health assistance to the region has declined by roughly 34%. In contrast, U.S. annual assessed contributions to PAHO have increased from $59.1 million in FY2009 to $65.7 million in FY2015. U.S. voluntary and assessed contributions currently represent roughly 37% of the organization's $200 million annual budget.[65] Despite these increases, PAHO has struggled to fund missions that bring experts to the region, which cost between $15,000 and $20,000 per expert. PAHO maintains that those missions, partnerships with NIH and other research entities, and training for health and vector control workers are greatly needed in the region.[66] The U.S. government also provides annually assessed and voluntary contributions to WHO, UNICEF, the World Bank, and the IDB, which have launched Zika responses in the region.

WHO and PAHO have launched a revised plan to support countries in their response to the Zika outbreak (see "WHO and PAHO," above) through 2017. As of mid-June 2016, WHO and PAHO have received $4 million to support what they estimate will cost $ 22 million overall.[67] The WHO has not reported voluntary contributions from the U.S. government for the plan, although the Administration's February 2016 Zika budget request includes $10 million for the WHO/PAHO response and the Administration reprogrammed $14 million of Ebola funds for voluntary contributions to WHO, PAHO, and UNICEF for Zika activities in April 2016.[68]

Given the relatively small U.S. health investment in the region (as discussed below), Congress may discuss the appropriate mix of funds, if any, to provide for multilateral Zika responses. In a region with relatively deep engagement with multilateral organizations, some would argue for providing increased funds to those entities. Others believe that it is harder to control how multilateral contributions are spent and ensure that related activities align with U.S. priorities.

Health as a Component of U.S. Assistance to Latin America and the Caribbean[69]

Current U.S. policy in Latin America is designed to promote economic and social opportunity, ensure the safety of the region's citizens, strengthen effective democratic institutions, and secure a clean energy future. As part of broader efforts to advance these priorities in the region, USAID and the State Department lead these efforts through a variety of foreign assistance programs. State Department assistance is primarily related to rule of law and security and certain other presidential priorities, whereas USAID focuses primarily on poverty alleviation, democracy and governance, health, and economic development. USAID and State Department assistance in Latin America and the Caribbean has been declining, particularly since FY2011—the period following

---

[65] CRS correspondence with PAHO official, June 10, 2016.

[66] NIH, "PAHO's Dr. Marcos Espinal on Global Partnerships to Fight Zika, Ebola, and Other Diseases," *Global Health Matters*, April 2016; CSIS, "2016 Global Development Forum."

[67] That estimate includes funds needed for a joint response by WHO/PAHO and some 60 partners. WHO, *Zika Strategic Response Plan Revised for July 2016-December 2017*, June 2016.

[68] USAID, "Zika Response: Initial Time-Critical Activities," April 6, 2016.

[69] For more information, see CRS Report R44113, *U.S. Foreign Assistance to Latin America and the Caribbean: Recent Trends and FY2016 Appropriations*, by Peter J. Meyer.

the release of the 2010 President's Policy Directive on Global Development (PPD-6).[70] Although the directive sought to elevate development as a "core pillar" of American foreign policy, it also directed U.S. agencies to "be more selective about where and in which sectors [they] work."

The PPD-6 prompted USAID to conduct a comprehensive review of its development assistance programs. Following a review of the health sector, USAID determined that many of the countries in the region "had achieved remarkable progress, were far ahead of other presence countries [i.e., those with a USAID mission], and could effectively sustain progress without further USAID assistance."[71] This finding led to a gradual reduction in health funding in the region (**Figure 4**). Health assistance fell from a high of $445.6 million in FY2010 to an estimated $231.3 million in FY2016.

Figure 4. U.S. Assistance to Latin America and the Caribbean: FY2009-FY2016

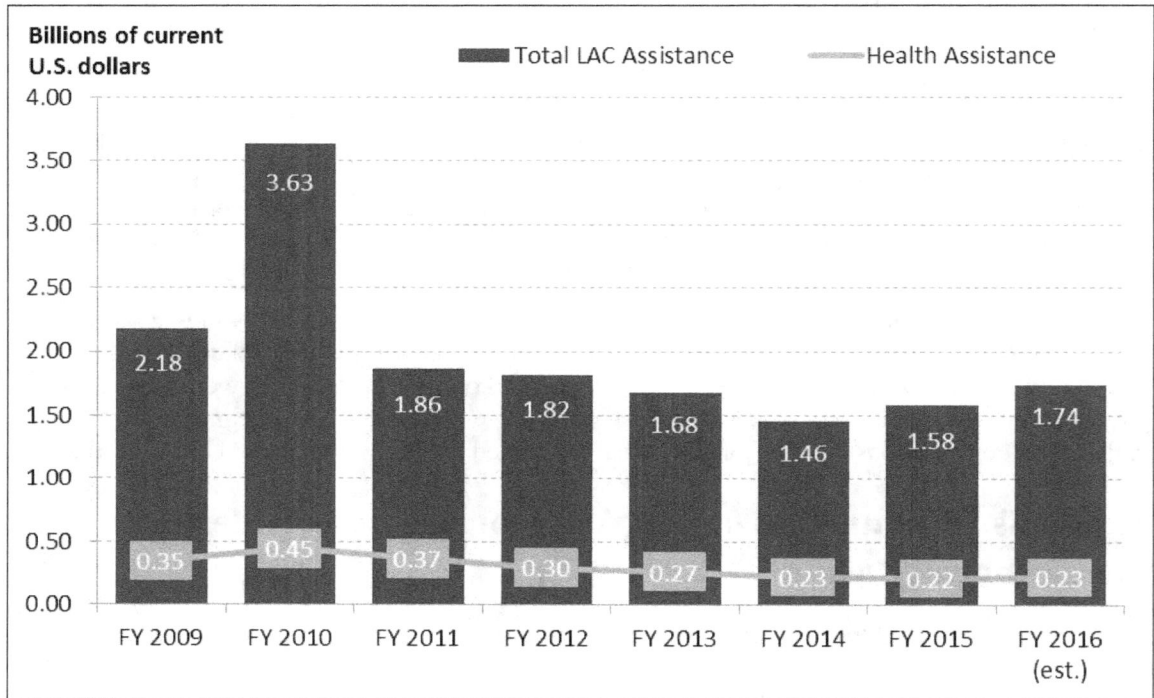

Source: U.S. Department of State, *Congressional Budget Justification for Foreign Operations*, FY2011-FY2017; Correspondence with USAID Budget Office, June 30, 2016.

Note: The FY2010 total includes $1.1 billion in supplemental appropriations, largely for Haiti in the aftermath of the earthquake. Health funds Include support from the State Department for HIV/AIDS programs funded through the President's Emergency Plan for AIDS Relief (PEPFAR).

---

[70] See White House, "U.S. Global Development Policy," September 22, 2010.

[71] CRS correspondence with USAID, June 8, 2016.

USAID continues to support programs related to maternal and child health, reproductive health, and family planning in Guatemala and Haiti, but it has discontinued such programs in all other countries across the region.[72] Policymakers concerned about development in Latin America may consider whether health should once again become a larger component of U.S. assistance programs, as inadequate access to health services can exacerbate poverty and inequality. A recent report by the U.N. Development Program urged governments and donors in the region to focus on addressing exclusion experienced by Afro-descendant and indigenous populations, women who suffer from domestic violence, and rural populations.[73] These issues may be of particular concern in Central America, where the Administration significantly increased development assistance in FY2016 (and in the FY2017 request) but did not include any funds for bilateral health programs in Honduras or El Salvador.

U.S. Global Health Support in Latin America

With support from USAID and other donors, many Latin American countries have made notable progress in improving the delivery of primary health care services—including access to contraception and basic prenatal care—over the past few decades. Since the 1960s, these developments have led to a 41% decline in maternal mortality, a 70% decline in infant mortality, and a drop in fertility rates from six children per family to between two and three children per family.[74]

---

[72] Jane T. Bertrand, *USAID Graduation From Family Planning Assistance: Implications for Latin America*, Population Institute and Tulane University School of Public Health and Tropical Medicine, October 2011; correspondence with USAID, June 8, 2016.

[73] U.N. Development Program, *Multidimensional Progress: Well-Being Beyond Income*, June 2016.

[74] Kimberly Cole, "A USAID Legacy in Latin America: Smaller Families and Better Health," *Frontlines*, July/August 2013.

Figure 5. USAID-Managed Global Health Funding in Latin America and the Caribbean: FY2009-FY2016

(current U.S. $ in millions and percentage)

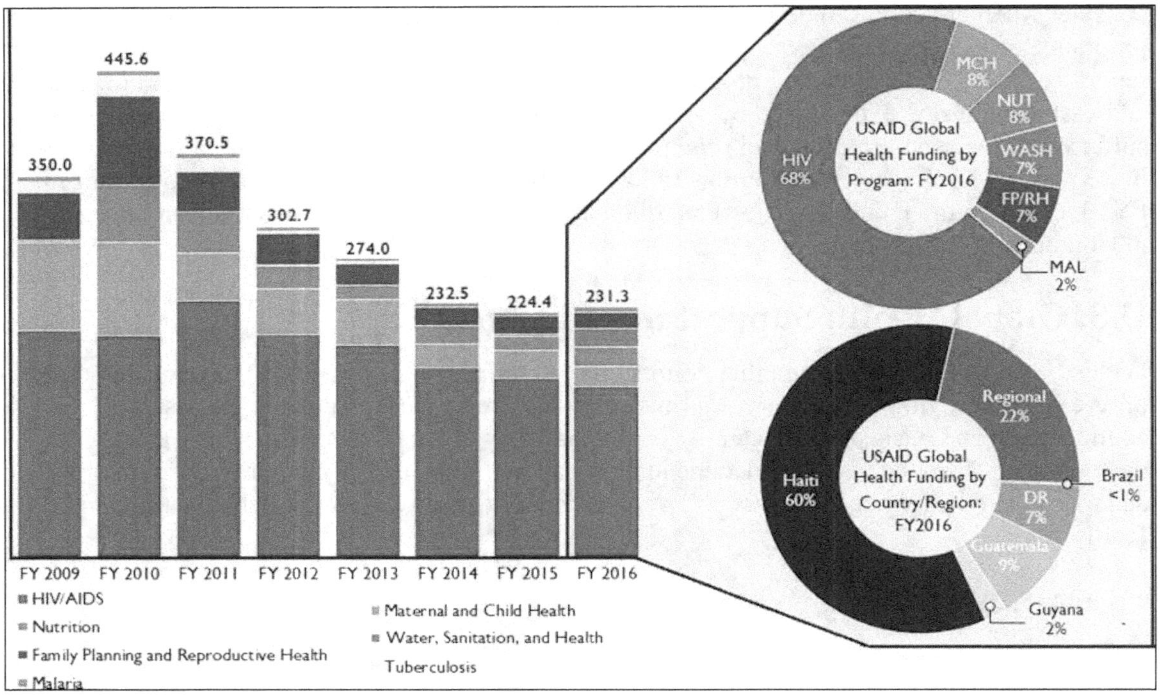

Source: Created by CRS from correspondence with USAID Budget Office, June 8, 2016.

Notes: FY2009-FY2015 are enacted levels and FY2016 is an estimate. MCH = maternal and child health; NUT = nutrition; WASH = water, sanitation, and hygiene; FP/RH = family planning/reproductive health; MAL = malaria; DR = Dominican Republic; Regional = regional programs. Some HIV/AIDS funding implemented by USAID is provided through a State Department account.

As a result of this progress, USAID global health engagement in the region has been steadily declining (see **Figure 5**). In FY2009, for example, USAID implemented global health programs in 14 countries in the region. By FY2016, USAID global health programs were operating in five countries (Brazil, Dominican Republic, Guatemala, Guyana, and Haiti). In three of those countries (Brazil, Dominican Republic, and Guyana), global health programs focus only on HIV/AIDS.[75] In FY2009, maternal and child health (23%) and reproductive health and family planning programs (13%) together constituted almost 40% of USAID health programs in Latin America. By 2016, maternal and child health (8%) and family planning and reproductive health programs (7%) amounted to 15% of all USAID health spending in the region.

In 2016, health ministers in several countries urged women to consider postponing pregnancy in response to Zika. Delaying or avoiding pregnancy is a problem in some communities where access to affordable and reliable contraception is limited and domestic violence (including spousal rape) is a major problem.[76] Experts estimate that some 56% of pregnancies in Latin America are unplanned, particularly among adolescents in poor communities who often do not

---

[75] Excludes regional programs in Latin America and the Caribbean that focus on HIV/AIDS.

[76] Sarah Bott et al., *Violence Against Women in Latin America and the Caribbean: A Comparative Analysis of Population-Based Data from 12 Countries*, PAHO, 2013.

have access to sexual education or counseling.[77] Health experts, including WHO Director-General Margaret Chan, have decried this constraint.[78] The WHO/PAHO Zika Strategic Response Plan urges support for reproductive health counseling and services, and pre- and postnatal care to pregnant women who may be affected by Zika and related birth defects.

Some groups have advocated for many countries in Latin America and the Caribbean to legalize abortions for severe microcephaly cases and have urged the United States to bolster investments in family planning and reproductive health services across the region.[79] Others oppose the legalization of abortion and argue that additional resources should be spent on finding effective treatments and vaccines. In February 2016, Pope Francis—an Argentinian who is influential in largely Catholic Latin America—indicated that birth control may be the "lesser evil" compared with allowing babies to be born with microcephaly, though he remained staunchly opposed to abortion.[80]

Pandemic Preparedness

In recent years, a succession of new and reemerging infectious diseases have caused outbreaks and pandemics that have together affected millions of people worldwide: Severe Acute Respiratory Syndrome (2003), Avian Influenza H5N1 (2005), Pandemic Influenza H1N1 (2009), Middle East Respiratory Syndrome coronavirus (2013), Ebola (2014), and Zika (2015). In 2014, former HHS Secretary Kathleen Sebelius and WHO Director-General Margaret Chan announced the Global Health Security Agenda (GHSA), a global effort to accelerate implementation of the International Health Regulations (2005), particularly in resource-poor countries that lack the ability to comply with the regulations.[81] The regulations include measures to strengthen global responses to public health events with potential international impact.

Some analysts have asserted that Zika transmission has exposed weaknesses in Latin American countries' pandemic preparedness.[82] As of 2012, PAHO maintained that only six countries (Brazil, Canada, Colombia, Costa Rica, and the United States) were prepared to handle a pandemic.[83] Through GHSA, the United States has committed to support 30 countries—two of which (Haiti and Peru) are in the Western Hemisphere—and CARICOM.[84]

Congress provided $597 million to CDC through emergency Ebola appropriations for the GHSA. The legislation did not specify where the funds were to be used. In light of the growing disease

---

[77] G. Sedgh, S. Singh, and R. Hussain, "Intended and Unintended Pregnancies Worldwide in 2012 and Recent Trends," *Studies in Family Planning*, no. 3 (September 2014), pp. 301-314.

[78] Margaret Chan, address to the 69th World Health Assembly, Geneva, Switzerland, May 23, 2016. See also Woodrow Wilson Center, "How Zika Is Shaping the Sexual and Reproductive Health and Rights Agenda," April 12, 2015.

[79] For current restrictions on U.S. family planning assistance, see CRS Report R41360, *Abortion and Family Planning-Related Provisions in U.S. Foreign Assistance Law and Policy*, by Luisa Blanchfield.

[80] "Full Text of Pope Francis' in-Flight Interview from Mexico to Rome," *Catholic News Agency*, February 18, 2016.

[81] For more information on GHSA, see CRS In Focus IF10022, *The Global Health Security Agenda and International Health Regulations*, by Tiaji Salaam-Blyther.

[82] Victor J. Dzau and Peter Sands, "Beyond the Ebola Battle—Winning the War Against Future Epidemics," *New England Journal of Medicine*, June 2016; Lawrence O. Goslin, "Neglected Dimensions of Global Security: The Global Health Risk Framework Commission," *Journal of the American Medical Association*, vol. 315, no. 12 (April 12, 2016).

[83] PAHO, September 2013.

[84] See the GHSA website at http://www.cdc.gov/globalhealth/security/ghsagenda.htm.

threats posed by *Aedes* mosquitoes in the Western Hemisphere, policymakers might consider whether to expand U.S. support for GHSA implementation to other countries in Latin America.

Given entreaties from health experts to bolster pandemic preparedness efforts to minimize the effects of future outbreaks, Congress might consider whether ongoing funding for pandemic preparedness is sufficient. Since FY2014, Congress has been appropriating $72.5 million annually to USAID and an average of $58 million annually to CDC for global health security efforts. The Administration is seeking $72.5 million for USAID and $65.2 million for CDC to implement global health security programs in FY2017.

Research and Development for Neglected Diseases

Since 2015, three disease outbreaks (dengue, chikungunya, and Zika) have spread from Latin America and the Caribbean into the United States, with the latter being only travel associated at the time of this report. These and other diseases lack vaccines to prevent transmission, treatment regimens, and effective vector control measures.

The WHO and other health experts have called for increasing investments in research and development for "neglected tropical diseases" such as dengue and chikungunya, as well as for Zika.[85] A consortium of health experts estimates that the international community would need to double current investments in health research and development for neglected diseases from $3 billion in 2014 to $6 billion by 2020 to meet global health goals.[86]

According to the Global Health Technologies Coalition, the United States accounts for roughly 70% of public investment and 45% of global investment in global health research and development.[87] The United States provides the highest amounts of funding for research and development for 26 of the 30 most neglected diseases. As of 2012, it supported more than half of the global health products in the development pipeline. Since peaking in 2009, however, U.S. funding for global health research and development has fluctuated (**Figure 6**).

---

[85] WHO, *Investing to Overcome the Global Impact of Neglected Tropical Diseases: Third WHO Report on Neglected Tropical Diseases*, February 2015; and Helen M. Lazear, Elizabeth M. Stringer, and Aravinda M. de Silva, "The Emerging Zika Virus Epidemic in the Americas: Research Priorities," *Journal of the American Medical Association*, May 10, 2016.

[86] Global Health Technologies Coalition, *Achieving a Bold Vision for Global Health: Policy Solutions to Advance Global Health R&D*, 2016, p. 6.

[87] Ibid.

Figure 6. U.S. Investment in Research and Development for Neglected Diseases

(2014 US$ in millions)

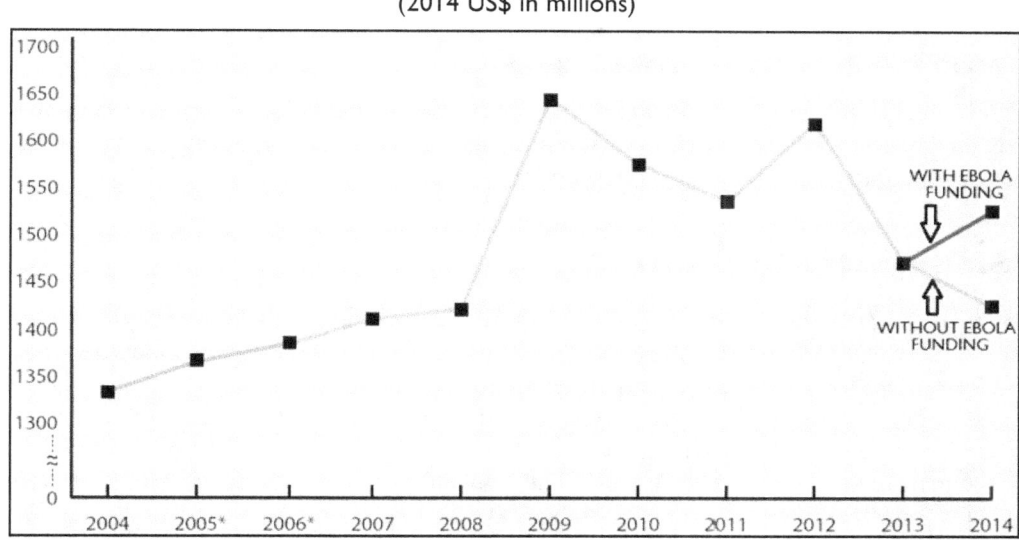

Source: Adapted by CRS from Global Health Technologies Coalition, *Achieving a Bold Vision for Global Health: Policy Solutions to Advance Global Health R&D*, 2016, p. 6.

Notes: Estimates. Data sources: Global Health Technologies Coalition, "Saving Lives and Creating Impact: Why Investing in Global Health Research Works," *Policy Cures*; 2012; and M. Moran et al., "Neglected Disease Research and Development: The Ebola Effect," *G-FINDER, Policy Cures*, 2015.

In April 2016, Congress enacted P.L. 114-146, Adding Zika Virus to the FDA Priority Review Voucher Program Act, to add the Zika virus to the list of tropical diseases eligible for the Food and Drug Administration's (FDA) Priority Review Voucher program, which allows companies to fast-track a product through the FDA regulatory process. It is unclear what effect this action will have on the development of products to control, treat, and prevent Zika, although several U.S. government agencies are already supporting development of vaccines and treatments for the Zika virus.[88] DOD is conducting preclinical research on a Zika vaccine candidate and plans to start human testing by the end of 2016. The Biomedical Advanced Research Development Authority (BARDA) within HHS has received a number of proposals to develop new Zika vaccines using vaccine platforms that could also be used for other emerging infectious disease threats. BARDA, NIH, and DOD are collaborating to support the development of a vaccine at DOD's Walter Reed Army Institute of Research.

Health experts argue that the Zika outbreak highlights the need to increase research not only for the treatment and prevention of human Zika infections but also for the development of effective vector control measures. At the 69th World Health Assembly, WHO Director-General Chan asserted that "the spread of Zika, the resurgence of dengue, and the emerging threat from chikungunya are the price being paid for a massive policy failure that dropped the ball on mosquito control in the 1970s."[89] Inappropriate and inconsistent use of insecticides has led to insecticide resistance and the growth of *Aedes* populations across the Western Hemisphere.[90] This

---

[88] See, for example, NIH, "NIAID Research Approach to Zika Virus," https://www niaid nih.gov/topics/zika/ResearchApproach/Pages/default.aspx; and DOD, "Walter Reed Scientists Test Zika Vaccine Candidate," June 10, 2016.

[89] Margaret Chan, "Address to the Sixty-Ninth World Health Assembly," May 23, 2016.

[90] Ildefonso Fernandez-Salas, "Historical Inability to Control *Aedes* Aegypti as a Main Contributor of Fast Dispersal of Chikungunya Outbreaks in Latin America," *Antiviral Research*, vol. 124 (October 27, 2015).

phenomenon has prompted some to advocate for increased U.S. investments in vector control in the region. Brazil has become the first country in the world to approve the large-scale use of genetically modified mosquitoes in vector control programs, and the FDA is reviewing a request to conduct trials of the technology in the United States.[91]

The Zika budget request includes $100 million for USAID to incentivize the development of Zika vaccines, diagnostics, and vector control measures. It is unclear whether these funds will be sufficient to encourage market development of these products.

Possible Future Actions

The future of the Zika supplemental funding request is uncertain at this time due to a number of controversial measures that are in the conference report. Some observers are concerned that there may not be enough time for the House and Senate to resume negotiations to reconcile their responses to the Zika outbreak before they adjourn in July.[92] In the meantime, U.S. agencies are using reprogrammed funds to complement current efforts by Latin American governments, PAHO, the private sector, and other donors. The size and scope of U.S.-funded initiatives to address Zika in Latin America and the Caribbean is also uncertain.

---

[91] For more information on genetically modified mosquitoes, see CRS In Focus IF10401, *Genetically Engineered Mosquitoes: A Vector Control Technology for Reducing Zika Virus Transmission*, by Tadlock Cowan.

[92] Kelsey Snell, "Zika Funding Bill Blocked in the Senate," *Washington Post*, June 28, 2016.

Appendix A. Supporting Documentation

Table A-1. Zika Funding Request

Department/Agency	Key Activities	Funding Level
Department of Health and Human Services (HHS)		**$1.509 billion**
U.S. Centers for Disease Control and Prevention (CDC)	• Support domestic Zika responses • Enhance domestic mosquito control programs • Establish domestic rapid response teams • Improve domestic laboratory and surveillance capacity • Expand the domestic CDC Pregnancy Risk Assessment Monitoring System, improve domestic Guillain-Barré syndrome tracking, and ensure the ability of domestic birth defect registries to detect Zika-related risks • Increase research linking Zika virus infections and microcephaly • Enhance international capacity for Zika surveillance, expand the Field Epidemiology Training Program (FETP), laboratory testing, health care provider training, and vector surveillance and control in countries at highest risk of Zika virus outbreaks • Improve diagnostics for Zika virus and support developments for vector control	$743 million, of which $150 million is for international efforts
Centers for Medicare and Medicaid Services	• Temporary one-year increase in Puerto Rico's Medicaid federal medical assistance percentage to support health services for pregnant women at risk of infection or diagnosed with Zika and for children with microcephaly and other related health costs	$250 million
Vaccine Research and Diagnostic Development and Procurement	• Research, rapid advanced development and commercialization of new vaccines and diagnostic tests for Zika virus	$200 million
	• Establish an Urgent and Emerging Threat Fund to address Zika and other outbreaks	$210 million
	• Support Puerto Rico's community health centers in preventing, screening, and treating Zika, expand home visiting services for low-income pregnant women at risk of Zika infection, and provide targeted maternal and child health services	
U.S. Agency for International Development (USAID)	• Implement vector management activities in countries at risk of Zika infection • Stimulate private sector research and development of vaccines, diagnostics, and vector control innovations • Support training of health care workers in affected countries • Support for pregnant women's health	**$335 million**

Department/Agency	Key Activities	Funding Level
	• Establish Zika education campaigns	
	• Issue a Global Health Security Grand Challenge calling for innovative diagnostics, vector control, personal protection, community engagement, and surveillance for Zika and other infectious diseases	
	• Provide flexibility in the use of remaining USAID Ebola funds	
U.S. Department of State	• Support for U.S. citizens and State Department employees in affected countries, public diplomacy, communications, and other operations activities	**$41 million**
	• Support World Health Organization and Pan American Health Organization efforts to minimize Zika threats in affected countries	

Source: White House, "Preparing for and Responding to the Zika Virus at Home and Abroad," February 8, 2016.

Notes: The FETP is CDC's program to train epidemiologists worldwide. For more information, see http://www.cdc.gov/globalhealth/healthprotection/fetp/index.htm.

Table A-2. Funding Redirected from USAID Ebola Emergency Operations for International Zika Responses

(current US$ in millions)

Department/Agency	Key Activities	Funding Level
USAID/U.S. Department of State	• Social and behavioral change communications	$17.0
	• Vector management	$50.0
	• Grand challenge for development	$30.0
	• Market incentives	$10.0
	• Maternal and child health interventions and service delivery	$17.0
	• Support for international organizations (PAHO, UNICEF)	$13.0
USAID Total		*$137.0*
CDC	• Implement Vector Management and Control	$7.0
	• Maternal and Child Health Interventions	$1.0
	• Innovations	$5.0
	• Surveillance, Epidemiology, and Studies	$44.0
	• Laboratory Capacity and Equipment	$15.0
	• Management and Coordination of Response	$6.0
CDC Total		*$78.0*

Source: USAID Congressional Notification, "Zika Response: Initial Time-Critical Activities," April 6, 2016.

Appendix B. Online Resources on Zika Virus

Organization	Source Title	Document/Link
Centers for Disease Control and Prevention (CDC)	Zika Travel Information	http://wwwnc.cdc.gov/travel/page/zika-travel-information
CDC	Zika Virus Index	http://www.cdc.gov/zika/index.html
Pan American Health Organization (PAHO)	Zika Resources for Health Authorities	http://www.paho.org/hq/index.php?option=com_content&view=article id=11601&Itemid=41694&lang=en
PAHO	Zika Resources for General Public	http://www.paho.org/hq/index.php?option=com_content&view=article id=11602&Itemid=41695&lang=en
PAHO	Epidemiological Alerts and Updates	http://www.paho.org/hq/index.php?option=com_content&view=article id=1239&Itemid=2291&lang=en
World Bank	Zika Virus Fact Sheet	http://www.worldbank.org/en/topic/health/brief/world-bank-group-and zika-fact-sheet
UNICEF, WHO, PAHO, IFRC	Risk communication and community engagement for Zika virus prevention and control	http://www.unicef.org/cbsc/files/ Zika_Virus_Prevention_and_Control_UNICEF_English.pdf
United Nations Population Fund (UNFPA)	Zika virus: Frequently asked questions	http://www.unfpa.org/resources/zika-virus-frequently-asked-questions
UNFPA	UNFPA on the Zika Virus Outbreak	http://www.unfpa.org/press/unfpa-zika-virus-outbreak
World Health Organization (WHO)	Zika Strategic Response Framework & Joint Operations Plan	http://apps.who.int/iris/bitstream/10665/204420/1/ ZikaResponseFramework_JanJun16_eng.pdf?ua=1
WHO	Zika Virus Situation Reports	http://who.int/emergencies/zika-virus/situation-report/en/

Author Contact Information

Clare Ribando Seelke, Coordinator
Specialist in Latin American Affairs
cseelke@crs.loc.gov, 7-5229

June S. Beittel
Analyst in Latin American Affairs
jbeittel@crs.loc.gov, 7-7613

Tiaji Salaam-Blyther
Specialist in Global Health
tsalaam@crs.loc.gov, 7-7677

Acknowledgments

Sarah A. Lister, Specialist in Public Health and Epidemiology, contributed a section on Zika in Puerto Rico and the U.S. Virgin Islands. Peter J. Meyer, Analyst in Latin American Affairs, contributed a section on Brazil and background on U.S. foreign assistance. Hannah Fischer, Information Research Specialist, and Amber Hope Wilhelm, Visual Information Specialist, provided graphics for this report. Edward Gracia, Research Associate, provided research support.

Supplemental Appropriations for Zika Response: The FY2016 Conference Agreement in Brief

Susan B. Epstein
Specialist in Foreign Policy

Sarah A. Lister
Specialist in Public Health and Epidemiology

July 14, 2016

Congressional Research Service
7-5700
www.crs.gov
R44549

Contents

Tables

Appendixes

Contacts

Background

The second session of the 114th Congress is considering whether and how to provide funds to control the spread of the Zika virus throughout the Americas. Zika infection, which is spread by *Aedes* mosquitoes, has been linked to birth defects and other health concerns. Local transmission of the virus has occurred in Puerto Rico, American Samoa, and the U.S. Virgin Islands and is expected on the U.S. mainland this summer, in areas where *Aedes* mosquitoes are present.

On February 22, 2016, the Obama Administration requested more than $1.89 billion in supplemental funding to respond to the Zika outbreak, all of which it requested as emergency discretionary appropriations and therefore effectively exempt from spending limits per the Budget Control Act of 2011 (BCA, P.L. 112-25).[1] The emergency request included $1.509 billion for the Department of Health and Human Services (HHS), $335 million for the U.S. Agency for International Development (USAID), and $41 million for the Department of State. The request also sought authority to transfer some of those supplemental emergency appropriations to other federal agencies such as the Department of Defense, the Environmental Protection Agency, and the U.S. Department of Agriculture, to allow greater flexibility as circumstances change. It also sought to provide HHS, the Department of State, and USAID with authority for direct hiring[2] and personal services contracting,[3] not limited to positions related to Zika response efforts.

On April 6, 2016, the White House Office of Management and Budget (OMB) and the Secretary of HHS announced that they had identified $589 million—$510 million of it from "existing Ebola resources within the Department of Health and Human Services and Department of State/USAID"—that could quickly be redirected and spent on immediate efforts to control and respond to the spread of the Zika virus in the Americas.[4] On April 8, 2016, the Administration notified Congress of the transfer of $295 million (included in the $510 million) from FY2015 unobligated USAID Ebola Economic Support Funds (ESF) to be used for the Zika response efforts. Of that amount, USAID would provide $158 million to CDC, including $78 million for Zika response and $80 million for Ebola response. The remaining $137 million would fund various USAID Zika response activities.[5]

In mid-May 2016, both the House and the Senate passed supplemental appropriations measures for Zika response. The House passed a stand-alone supplemental appropriations bill (H.R. 5243) on May 18. This bill would provide $622.1 million in Zika funding, which would be available until September 30, 2016, and also rescinded an equal amount of budget authority. The Senate voted to amend the combined FY2017 Military Construction-Veterans Affairs and Transportation-Housing and Urban Development appropriations bills (S.Amdt. 3900 to H.R. 2577, passed on May 19) to provide $1.1 billion in Zika response funding, which would be available, depending

---

[1] White House, Office of Management and Budget, "Estimate #1 – FY 2016 Emergency Supplemental: Appropriations Request to Respond to the Zika Virus both Domestically and Internationally," February 22, 2016, https://www.whitehouse.gov/omb/budget_amendments.

[2] For more detail, see https://www.opm.gov/blogs/Director/direct-hire-authority/.

[3] As defined in regulation, "The Government is normally required to obtain its employees by direct hire under competitive appointment or other procedures required by the civil service laws. Obtaining personal services by contract, rather than by direct hire, circumvents those laws unless Congress has specifically authorized acquisition of the services by contract." (48 C.F.R. 37.104(a)) Under this authority, federal agencies can quickly contract with individual scientists, physicians, and other experts to aid in response efforts.

[4] OMB, Shaun Donovan, "Taking Every Step Necessary, As Quickly as Possible, to Protect the American People from Zika," OMB blog, April 6, 2016, https://www.whitehouse.gov/omb/blog.

[5] In the absence of detailed information about these reprogrammings, they are not presented in Table 1.

on the account, until September 30, 2017, or until expended. Unlike the House bill, the Senate Zika proposal only rescinded $10 million.

On June 22, 2016, Harold Rogers, chairman of the House Appropriations Committee, filed a conference agreement. (See the "conference report," H.Rept. 114-640, to accompany H.R. 2577.) The conference agreement (Division B) would provide $1.1 billion in Zika response funding. Amounts to HHS and State/USAID accounts are somewhat similar to those in the Senate proposal. However, a provision that specifies the uses of funds provided to the Social Services Block Grant (SSBG) has proven controversial. The conference agreement provides that SSBG funds may only be used for health services "provided by public health departments, hospitals, or reimbursed through public health plans," which some have argued could prevent these funds from going to other entities that offer family planning and women's health services.[6] Also, the agreement (Division D) would rescind $750 million in budget authority, the majority of it from unspent funds in the Patient Protection and Affordable Care Act (ACA, P.L. 111-148, as amended) intended to establish health exchanges in the territories.[7] The Administration has stated its objection to the controversial reproductive health care provision and the ACA offset.[8]

The conference agreement was approved by the House on June 23, 2016. On June 28, the Senate voted (52-48) not to invoke cloture on the conference agreement. Subsequent discussions among Members of Congress and the Administration did not yield an alternative agreement. The Administration sent a letter to congressional leaders on July 12, a few days before a planned seven-week congressional recess, urging them to provide Zika supplemental funding, and citing examples of activities that could be compromised without it.[9] Some Members were concerned, however, that much of the funds reprogrammed by the Administration in April had not yet been obligated, and urged the Administration to make use of funds already available to it. On July 14, before adjourning for a seven-week recess, the Senate again voted (52-44) not to invoke cloture on the conference agreement.

For More Information

This CRS report presents funding proposals for response to the Zika outbreak, including proposals in Division B of the conference report, and, where applicable, associated proposed rescissions, including those in Division D of the conference report. Division A, Military Construction and Veterans Affairs and Related Agencies Appropriations for FY2017 (MILCON-VA appropriations), is not discussed in this CRS report.[10] Division C of the conference report

---

[6] Ali Rogin, "Senate Zika Bill Falls Apart Largely over Planned Parenthood Objections," *ABC News*, June 28, 2016, http://abcnews.go.com/Politics/senate-zika-bill-falls-largely-planned-parenthood-objections/story?id=40193006.

[7] Section 1323(a) of the ACA provides that each U.S. territory can either elect to establish a health insurance exchange by October 1, 2013 and receive a portion of a $1 billion appropriation to do so, or increase its Medicaid funding. For more information, see CRS Report R44275, *Puerto Rico and Health Care Finance: Frequently Asked Questions*, coordinated by Annie L. Mach. No U.S. territory elected to establish a health insurance exchange. Section 101 of the conference report would rescind $543 million from the $1 billion appropriation.

[8] White House, Statement by Press Secretary Josh Earnest on the Zika Conference Report, June 22, 2016, https://www.whitehouse.gov/briefing-room/statements-and-releases.

[9] The letter is available from the article by Jennifer Shutt, "Senate Again Rejects Moving to a Vote on Zika, Veterans Funding," *CQ News*, July 14, 2016.

[10] Division A does not include an earlier MILCON-VA provision on display of the Confederate Flag. For more information, see CRS Insight IN10313, *Display of the Confederate Flag at Federal Cemeteries in the United States*, by Laura B. Comay and Scott D. Szymendera.

addresses the Environmental Protection Agency's (EPA's) regulation of water pollution and pesticides, and is beyond the scope of this CRS report.[11]

For more information about the Zika virus outbreak, see the following CRS reports:

- CRS Report R44460, *Zika Response Funding: Request and Congressional Action*, for more information about the supplemental request for Zika response appropriations, and unobligated funds for the Ebola response. (This report will be updated to include any final action taken by the 114th Congress);

- CRS Insight IN10433, *Zika Virus: Global Health Considerations*, for information about U.S. assistance for international response to the outbreak; and

- CRS Report R44545, *Zika Virus in Latin America and the Caribbean: U.S. Policy Considerations*.

See also the following Web pages on the Zika outbreak:

- Centers for Disease Control and Prevention (CDC), https://www.cdc.gov/zika/;

- World Health Organization (WHO), http://www.who.int/topics/zika/en/; and

- Pan American Health Organization (PAHO), http://www.paho.org/hq/index.php?option=com_content&view=article&id=11585&Itemid=41688&lang=en.

Comparison of Funding Proposals

Table 1 below presents a comparison of amounts for response to the Zika outbreak proposed in the Administration's supplemental request, by the House and Senate, and in the conference agreement. **Table 2**, below, presents a comparison of selected non-monetary provisions in these measures. The **Appendix** lists acronyms used in the tables.

Table 1. Supplemental FY2016 Funding for Zika Response: Comparison of Administration Request with Senate, House, and Conference Proposals

Budget Authority in $ Millions

Agency/Program	Request	S.Amdt. 3900	H.R. 5243	Conf. Rept., H.R. 2577, Div. B
HRSA: Community Health Centers	0.0	40.0	0.0	0.0
HRSA: National Health Service Corps	0.0[a]	6.0	0.0	0.0
HRSA: Maternal and Child Health Block Grant	0.0[a]	5.0	0.0[b]	0.0
HRSA Subtotal	0.0	51.0	0.0	0.0
PHSSEF: Social Services Block Grant	0.0	75.0	0.0	95.0
PHSSEF: Primary Care	not specified	0.0	0.0	46.0[c]
PHSSEF: Community Health Centers	not specified	0.0	0.0	40.0[c]
PHSSEF: National Health Service Corps	not specified	0.0	0.0	6.0[c]

---

[11] For more information, see CRS Report RL32884, *Pesticide Use and Water Quality: Are the Laws Complementary or in Conflict?*, by Claudia Copeland.

Agency/Program	Request	S.Amdt. 3900	H.R. 5243	Conf. Rept., H.R. 2577, Div. B
PHSSEF: Maternal and Child Health Block Grant	*not specified*	*0.0*	*0.0b*	*0.0*
PHSSEF: Medical Countermeasure and Other	*not specified*	*75.0*	*103.0*	*85.0*
PHSSEF Subtotal	295.0	150.0	103.0	227.0
CDC	828.0	449.0	170.0db	476.0
NIH/NIAID	130.0	200.0	230.0	230.0
FDAe	10.0	0.0	0.0	0.0
CMS (Medicaid federal matching rate)	246.0	no provision	no provision	no provision
HHS Total	**1,509.0**	**850.0**	**503.0**	**933.0**
State: Diplomatic and Consular Programs (D&CP)	14.6	14.6	9.1f	14.6
State: Emergencies in the Diplomatic and Consular Service	4.0	4.0	0.0g	4.0
State: Repatriation Loans	1.0	1.0	0.0	1.0
State: Nonproliferation, Anti-Terrorism, Demining and Related Programs (NADR)	8.0	4.0	0.0	0.0
State: International Organizations and Programs (IO&P)	13.5	13.5	0.0	0.0
USAID: Operating Expenses (OE)	10.0	10.0	10.0	10.0
USAID: Global Health Programs (GHP)	325.0	211.0	100.0h	145.0
State/USAID Total	**376.1**	**258.1**	**119.1**	**174.6**
REQUEST OR BILL TOTAL	**1,885.1**	**1,108.1**	**622.1**	**1,107.6**
Rescission: USAID, unobligated Ebola OE	0.0	-10.0	0.0	-10.0i
Rescission: Other Ebola unobligated balances	0.0	0.0	-352.1	-107.0
Rescission: HHS, Non-recurring Expenses Fund	0.0	0.0	-270.0	-100.0
Rescission: HHS, Affordable Care Act (ACA)	0.0	0.0	0.0	-543.0i
Total Rescissions	**0.0**	**-10.0**	**-622.1**	**-760.0**
NET TOTAL BUDGET AUTHORITY	**1,885.1**	**1,098.1**	**0.0**	**347.6**

Sources: CRS analysis of text of White House, Office of Management and Budget, "Estimate #1–FY 2016 Emergency Supplemental: Appropriations Request to Respond to the Zika Virus both Domestically and Internationally," February 22, 2016, https://www.whitehouse.gov/omb/budget_amendments; S.Amdt. 3900; H.R. 5243 IH; and H.Rept. 114-640, to accompany H.R. 2577.

Notes: Requested amounts reflect the initial request of February 2016, and do not reflect reprogramming of funds in April 2016. Details may not add to totals due to rounding. Amounts in italics add to subtotals.

a. Unspecified amounts from the PHSSEF may be transferred to HRSA for National Health Service Corps activities in the territories, and for the MCH Block Grant.

b. Up to $50.0 million of the CDC funds provided may be transferred to HRSA Maternal and Child Health Services (MCH) Block Grant for specified activities.

c. These funds would be transferred to HRSA for the specified activities.

d. Of the CDC funds provided, up to $500,000 each must be transferred to the HHS Office of Inspector General and the Comptroller General for oversight activities.

e. The House-reported Agriculture and Related Agencies appropriation for FY2017 included $10 million for FDA activities related to the response to Ebola, Zika, and other emerging threats. H.Rept. 114-531, p. 70.

f. Up to $1.35 million of funds for Diplomatic and Consular Services may be used for medical evacuation costs for any U.S. agency.

g. Up to $1.0 million of funds for Diplomatic and Consular Services may be transferred to Emergencies in the Diplomatic and Consular Service

h. Of the Global Health Program funds provided, up to $500,000 each must be transferred to the USAID Office of Inspector General and the Comptroller General for oversight activities.

i. Div. B of the conference report would rescind these funds previously appropriated for Ebola activities within Division J of P.L. 113-235.

j. Section 1323(a) of the ACA provides that each U.S. territory can either elect to establish a health insurance exchange by October 1, 2013 and receive a portion of a $1 billion appropriation to do so, or increase its Medicaid funding. For more information, see CRS Report R44275, *Puerto Rico and Health Care Finance: Frequently Asked Questions*, coordinated by Annie L. Mach. No U.S. territory elected to establish a health insurance exchange. Section 101 of H.Rept. 114-640 would rescind $543 million from the $1 billion appropriation.

Table 2. Selected Provisions for Zika Response in FY2016 Supplemental: Comparison of Administration Request, Senate and House Proposals, and Conference Report

Provision(s)	Administration Request	Senate (S.Amdt. 3900)	House (H.R. 5243 IH)	Conference Report (H.R. 2577)
Period of Availability of Funds				
HHS Funds	Until expended.	Until Sept. 30, 2017.	Until Sept. 30, 2016.	Until Sept. 30, 2017.
State/USAID Funds: D&CP: Nonproliferation, Anti-Terrorism, Demining and Related Programs; International Organizations and Programs; Operating Expenses	Until Sept. 30, 2017.	Until Sept. 30, 2017.	Until Sept. 30, 2016.	Until Sept. 30, 2017.
State/USAID Funds: Emergencies in the Diplomatic and Consular Service; Repatriation Loans; Global Health Programs.	Until expended.	Until expended.	Until Sept. 30, 2016.	Until Sept. 30, 2017.
Oversight funds for HHS and International Affairs	No comparable provision.	Until expended.	Until expended.	Until expended.
Authority to Reimburse Prior Obligations				
HHS and State/USAID Funds	Any funds in this Act may be used to reimburse HHS and/or State/USAID accounts for obligations incurred for Zika virus response prior to enactment	$88 million may be used to reimburse CDC accounts for obligations incurred for Zika virus response prior to enactment.	No authority to reimburse prior obligations.	$88 million may be used to reimburse CDC accounts for obligations incurred for Zika virus response prior to enactment.
Scope of Use of Funds				
CDC Funds	To prevent, prepare for, and respond to Zika virus, other vector-borne diseases, or other infectious diseases and related health outcomes,	To prevent, prepare for, and respond to Zika virus, other vector-borne diseases, and related health outcomes, domestically and	To prevent, prepare for, and respond to Zika virus, domestically and internationally.	To prevent, prepare for, and respond to Zika virus, health conditions related to such virus, and other vector-borne diseases,

Provision(s)	Administration Request	Senate (S.Amdt. 3900)	House (H.R. 5243 IH)	Conference Report (H.R. 2577)
	domestically and internationally.	internationally.		domestically and internationally
Use of CDC funds for grants pursuant to PHSA §317S, the Mosquito Abatement for Safety and Health (MASH) Act, which allows direct funding to local jurisdictions.	Permitted, as determined by the CDC Director to be appropriate.	Not permitted.	Permitted, as determined by the CDC Director to be appropriate.	Permitted, as determined by the CDC Director to be appropriate.
HRSA Funds	Scope for PHSSEF funds would apply to any funds transferred to HRSA.	To prevent, prepare for, and respond to Zika virus, other vector-borne diseases, and related health outcomes, domestically and internationally.	Scope for CDC funds would apply to any funds transferred to HRSA.	Scope for PHSSEF funds would apply to any funds transferred to HRSA.
NIH Funds	To prevent, prepare for, and respond to Zika virus, other vector-borne diseases, or other infectious diseases and related health outcomes, domestically and internationally.	To prevent, prepare for, and respond to Zika virus, other vector-borne diseases, and related health outcomes, domestically and internationally.	For development of vaccines for the Zika virus.	For specified research and medical countermeasures development regarding Zika virus and other vector-borne diseases, domestically and internationally.
PHSSEF Funds	To prevent, prepare for, and respond to Zika virus, other vector-borne diseases, or other infectious diseases and related health outcomes, domestically and internationally.	To prevent, prepare for, and respond to Zika virus, other vector-borne diseases, and related health outcomes, domestically and internationally.	To respond to Zika virus, domestically and internationally.	To prevent, prepare for, and respond to Zika virus, health conditions related to such virus, and other vector- borne diseases, domestically and internationally.
State Dept. Diplomatic and Consular Programs (D&CP)	To support response efforts related to the Zika virus and related health outcomes, other vector-borne diseases, or other infectious diseases.	To support response efforts related to the Zika virus and related health outcomes, other vector-borne diseases, or other infectious diseases.	To support cost of medical evacuations and other response efforts related to the Zika virus and health conditions directly associated with the Zika virus.	To support response efforts related to the Zika virus, related health conditions, and other vector-borne diseases.
State Dept. Emergencies in Diplomatic and Consular Service	To support response efforts related to the Zika virus and related health outcomes, other vector-borne diseases.	To support response efforts related to the Zika virus and related health outcomes, other vector-borne diseases.	No comparable provision.	To support response efforts related to the Zika virus, related health conditions, and other vector-borne diseases.
Repatriation Loans Program	For direct loans to support response efforts related to the Zika virus and related health outcomes, other vector-borne diseases, or other infectious diseases.	For direct loans to support response efforts related to the Zika virus and related health outcomes, other vector-borne diseases, or other infectious diseases.	No comparable provision.	For direct loans to support response efforts related to the Zika virus, related health conditions, and other vector-borne diseases.
USAID Operating Expenses	To support response	To support response	Response efforts	To support response

Provision(s)	Administration Request	Senate (S.Amdt. 3900)	House (H.R. 5243 IH)	Conference Report (H.R. 2577)
(OE)	efforts related to the Zika virus and related health outcomes, other vector-borne diseases, or other infectious diseases.	efforts related to the Zika virus and related health outcomes, other vector-borne diseases, or other infectious diseases.	related to the Zika virus and health conditions directly associated with the Zika virus.	efforts related to the Zika virus, related health conditions, and other vector-borne diseases.
Global Health Programs (GHP)	For assistance or research to prevent, treat, or otherwise respond to the Zika virus and related health outcomes, other vector-borne diseases, or other infectious diseases.	For assistance or research to prevent, treat, or otherwise respond to the Zika virus and related health outcomes, other vector-borne diseases, or other infectious diseases.	For vector control activities to prevent, prepare for, and respond to the Zika virus internationally.	For expenses to prevent, prepare for, and respond to the Zika virus, related health conditions, and other vector-borne diseases.
Dept. of State, Nonproliferation, Anti-terrorism, Demining and Related Programs (NADR)	To support response and research efforts related to the Zika virus and related health outcomes, other vector-borne diseases, or other infectious diseases.	To support response and research efforts related to the Zika virus and related health outcomes, other vector-borne diseases, or other infectious diseases.	No comparable provision.	No comparable provision.
International Organizations and Programs (IO&P)	To support response and research efforts related to the Zika virus and related health outcomes, other vector-borne diseases, or other infectious diseases.	To support response and research efforts related to the Zika virus and related health outcomes, other vector-borne diseases, or other infectious diseases.	No comparable provision.	No comparable provision.
Transfer Authority				
HHS Funds	CDC funds may be transferred within CDC. NIH funds may be transferred within NIH. PHSSEF funds may be transferred to two stated HRSA accounts, as specified, to an HHS countermeasures injury compensation fund, and to any other HHS accounts.	Any HHS funds in the amendment may be transferred to accounts in CDC, HRSA, NIH, and PHSSEF. $75 million in PHSSEF funds must be transferred to the HHS Social Services Block Grant.	CDC funds may be transferred within CDC, and to three stated HRSA accounts, as specified. NIH funds may be transferred within NIH. PHSSEF funds may be transferred to an HHS countermeasures injury compensation fund.	HHS Funds may be transferred and merged with CDC, PHSSEF, and NIH funds for purposes specified in this title following consultation with OMB. PHSSEF funds may be transferred to an HHS countermeasures injury compensation fund.
International Affairs	Funds may be transferred between foreign affairs accounts within the same headings to carry out the purposes of this Act and are in addition to other transfer authority within this proposal.	Funds within certain foreign affairs accounts may be transferred between foreign affairs accounts within the same headings to carry out the purposes of this Act and are in addition to other transfer authority within this proposal.	Specified funds within D&CP may be transferred for medical evacuation, transferred for Emergencies in Diplomatic and Consular Service, and are in addition to any other transfer authority within this	Funds for D&CP, Emergencies in Diplomatic and Consular Service, Repatriation Loans Program, and OE may be transferred to funds under such headings to carry out the purposes of the title, are in addition to other

Provision(s)	Administration Request	Senate (S.Amdt. 3900)	House (H.R. 5243 IH)	Conference Report (H.R. 2577)
			proposal.	transfer authority provided by law, and require 5 day prior notification in writing to the appropriations committees.

Notification, Reporting and Oversight

Provision(s)	Administration Request	Senate (S.Amdt. 3900)	House (H.R. 5243 IH)	Conference Report (H.R. 2577)
HHS Notification Requirement for Obligation	No comparable provision.	No comparable provision.	15 days in advance of obligation.	No comparable provision.
International Affairs Notification Requirement for Obligation	No comparable provision.	15 days in advance of obligation.	15 days in advance of obligation.	15 days in advance of obligation.
HHS Reporting Requirement	No comparable provision.	Within 30 days of enactment the HHS Secretary must report to the Appropriations Committees with a spend plan, followed by quarterly reports on obligations until funds have been fully expended.	Within 30 days of enactment the HHS Secretary must report to the Appropriations Committees with a spend plan, which must be updated and resubmitted every 30 days until funds have been fully expended.	Within 30 days after enactment the HHS Secretary must report to the Appropriations Committees with a spend plan, updated every 60 days until September 30, 2017.
International Affairs Reporting Requirement	No comparable provision.	Within 45 days after enactment and prior to obligation of international funds, the USAID Administrator must submit spend plans to the Committees on Appropriations, update and resubmit to those committees every 90 days until September 30, 2017, and every 180 days thereafter until all funds are expended.	Within 30 days after enactment the Secretary of State and USAID Administrator must submit to Appropriations Committees a consolidated report and update and submitted to those committees every 30 days until all funds are expended.	Within 30 days after enactment the Secretary of State and USAID Administrator must submit to the Appropriations Committees a consolidated report, including anticipated uses of funds, on a country and project basis, including estimated personnel and administrative costs, and updated every 60 days until September 30, 2017.
HHS: Oversight of Funded Activities	No comparable provision.	No comparable provision.	$500,000 of CDC funds must be made available to the HHS Office of the Inspector General. An additional $500,000 of CDC funds must be made available to the Comptroller General.	$500,000 of PHSSEF funds must be made available to the HHS Office of the Inspector General. An additional $500,000 of PHSSEF funds must be made available to the Comptroller General.
International Affairs: Oversight of Funded Activities	No comparable provision.	$500,000 from the International Affairs Chapter must be made available to the	$500,000 from GHP funds must be made available to USAID's Office of the	$500,000 within the international title must be transferred to USAID's Office of the

Provision(s)	Administration Request	Senate (S.Amdt. 3900)	House (H.R. 5243 IH)	Conference Report (H.R. 2577)
		Comptroller General.	Inspector General.	Inspector General.
			An additional $500,000 from GHP funds must be made available to the Comptroller General.	An additional $500,000 must be made available to the Comptroller General.

Source: CRS analysis of text of White House, Office of Management and Budget, "Estimate #1–FY 2016 Emergency Supplemental: Appropriations Request to Respond to the Zika Virus both Domestically and Internationally," February 22, 2016, https://www.whitehouse.gov/omb/budget_amendments; S.Amdt. 3900; H.R. 5243 IH; and Conference Report (H.Rept. 114-640).

Appendix. Glossary

ACA—Patient Protection and Affordable Care Act, P.L. 111-148, as amended

BCA—Budget Control Act of 2011, P.L. 112-25

CDC—Centers for Disease Control and Prevention (HHS)

CMS—Centers for Medicare & Medicaid Services

D&CP—Diplomatic and Consular Programs

FDA—Food and Drug Administration

FAO—Food and Agriculture Organization

GHP—Global Health Programs

HHS—Department of Health and Human Services

HRSA—Health Resources and Services Administration (HHS)

ESF—Economic Support Funds

IAEA—International Atomic Energy Agency

NIAID—National Institute of Allergy and Infectious Diseases (NIH)

NIH—National Institutes of Health (HHS)

OE—Operating Expenses

OIG—Office of Inspector General

PAHO—Pan American Health Organization

PHSSEF—Public Health and Social Services Emergency Fund

PHSA—Public Health Service Act

SSBG—Social Services Block Grant

USAID—U.S. Agency for International Development

UNICEF—United Nations Children's Fund

WHO—World Health Organization

Author Contact Information

Susan B. Epstein
Specialist in Foreign Policy
sepstein@crs.loc.gov, 7-6678

Sarah A. Lister
Specialist in Public Health and Epidemiology
slister@crs.loc.gov, 7-7320

Acknowledgments

The authors acknowledge the assistance of Grant D. Clinkingbeard, Research Associate; Elayne J. Heisler, Specialist in Health Services; Karen E. Lynch, Specialist in Social Policy; Annie L. Mach, Specialist in Health Care Financing; Alison Mitchell, Specialist in Health Care Financing; Angela Napili, Senior Research Librarian; Jon O. Shimabukuro, Legislative Attorney; and Jessica Tollestrup, Specialist in Social Policy, in the preparation of this report.

Mosquito Control in the United States

Mosquitoes and the diseases they transmit are in the news in the summer of 2016. Although *Aedes* mosquitoes and the Zika virus make headlines, health officials must sustain their efforts against other mosquito-borne threats such as West Nile virus (WNV). WNV is spread by *Culex* and other kinds of mosquitoes and has been reported in each of the lower 48 states and Puerto Rico. In 2015, WNV caused more than 1,300 severe illnesses and more than 100 deaths in the United States. In the absence of vaccines against most mosquito-borne infections, mosquito control is a key public health tool.

Conventional Mosquito Control

Different types of mosquitoes necessitate different control approaches. (See CRS In Focus IF10353, *Mosquitoes, Zika Virus, and Transmission Ecology*, for more information.) However, these approaches all involve three or more of the five prongs of conventional mosquito control.

- **Surveillance:** trapping and sorting to show which mosquito species are present, and testing them for disease-causing viruses and bacteria.

Figure 1. Tires Are Ideal Habitats for Mosquitoes

Staff with the Greater Los Angeles County Vector Control District sample water in a discarded tire for mosquito larvae.

Source: The Greater Los Angeles County Vector Control District, http://www.glacvcd.org/.

- **Source reduction:** the removal of standing water, in which mosquitoes breed. Different mosquito species favor different water habitats. For example, *Aedes* mosquitoes are often "small container" breeders, using water that collects in bottlecaps, grocery bags, and other common trash items.

- **Larvicidal treatment:** the use of pesticides registered by the Environmental Protection Agency (EPA) under the Federal Insecticide, Fungicide, and Rodenticide Act (7 U.S.C. §136 et seq.) to kill mosquitoes in the young (larval) stage, when they live in water. Larvicides are applied to water sources directly or by aerial spraying.

- **Adulticidal treatment:** the use of EPA-registered pesticides to kill adult (flying) mosquitoes. This is often done by aerial spraying.

- **Public education and outreach:** messaging about the importance of source reduction around the home, ways to avoid being bitten (e.g., appropriate repellants and clothing), and other important individual actions.

Surveillance, source reduction, and outreach are useful for any type of mosquito control problem. Depending on the mosquito species of concern and other factors, pesticide use may or may not be an effective addition to control efforts.

(This information is drawn from the Centers for Disease Control and Prevention, or CDC, at http://www.cdc.gov/zika/vector/index html. Newer mosquito control technologies are beyond the scope of this report. For more information, see CRS In Focus IF10401, *Genetically Engineered Mosquitoes: A Vector Control Technology for Reducing Zika Virus Transmission*.)

Current Mosquito Control Infrastructure

In the United States, mosquito control (often called "abatement") is the responsibility of a patchwork of different entities. Some states retain special districts that coordinate, fund, and carry out mosquito control activities locally. Some states coordinate mosquito control activities statewide under one of several umbrellas—public health, agriculture, parks and recreation, environmental quality, or some other state agency. Funding sources also vary and may include property assessments, taxes on vehicle tires, and other approaches, often in lieu of appropriated funds.

Although CRS has not identified a comprehensive description of the nation's mosquito control infrastructure, numerous anecdotal reports suggest the system is not merely variable, but may also be fragmented and incomplete. Some localities are well prepared, with aircraft, trucks, and dedicated operational budgets. Other equally vulnerable localities do not appear to have the personnel or equipment needed to conduct effective mosquito control activities, or to expand such activities in response to a new threat.

In a lot of places, it's one guy in the community who drives a snow plow in the winter and picks up [a] fogger in the summer.

Paul Ettestad of the New Mexico health department at a CDC-sponsored Zika summit. Lena H. Sun, "As Mosquito Season Arrives, Is the U.S. Ready for Zika?" *Washington Post*, April 1, 2016.

The National Pesticide Information Center (NPIC), a collaboration of Oregon State University and the EPA to provide pesticide-related information, keeps a list of contact agencies or persons for vector or mosquito control by U.S. county, as reported to NPIC. ("Vector" refers to a living organism, such as a mosquito, that transmits a disease to another living organism.) **Figure 2** shows counties with a reported contact in black, and those without in white. Although some of the white area may represent under-reporting, the map nonetheless appears to show that some localities lack coordinated mosquito control programs.

(Of note, the federal government is responsible for vector control on federal lands. Also, coordinated vector control may not be needed in minimally populated areas or over large bodies of water.)

Figure 2. Vector Control Contacts Reported to NPIC

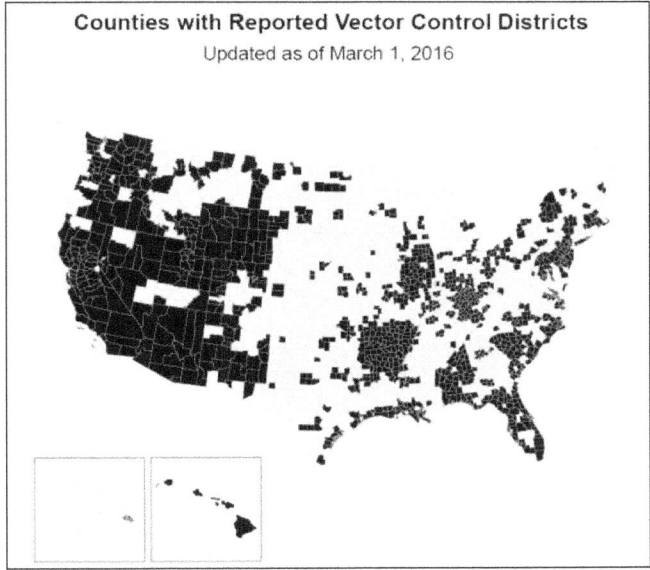

Counties with Reported Vector Control Districts

Updated as of March 1, 2016

Source: National Pesticide Information Center (NPIC), "Find Your Local Resources," http://npic.orst.edu/mlr.html.

Federal Grants for Mosquito Control

Although a variety of state agencies may support mosquito control efforts, grants from the CDC appear to be the only consistent source of federal assistance to states for these efforts. Funding from two CDC flexible capacity grants has been used to control mosquitoes that transmit diseases of public health concern (in contrast to mosquitoes that are merely "nuisance" biters). These are the Public Health Emergency Preparedness (PHEP) Cooperative Agreements (a type of grant), and the Epidemiology and Laboratory Capacity (ELC) grants. Each of these grants provides annual awards to the health departments in all 50 states, the territories, the District of Columbia, and several large U.S. cities for a wide array of public health preparedness and infrastructure needs.

Grantees may use PHEP and ELC funds for elements of mosquito control as part of a broader CDC-approved application and spending plan. Historically, funds could be used for mosquito surveillance and public education/outreach, but not necessarily for other "operational" activities (i.e., source reduction or pesticide treatments).

In the spring of 2016, CDC announced the availability of $85 million in public health emergency and ELC funding to address the Zika virus threat. Accompanying guidance said that grantees may use funds for vector control if local mosquito-borne Zika virus transmission is occurring, but did not state specific allowable activities. In its "Draft Zika Interim Response Plan" of June 14, 2016, CDC said it plans to deploy federal assistance to grantees through CDC Emergency Response Teams (CERT teams)—vector control specialists who can assist with mosquito surveillance, monitor mosquito density during control activities, and test mosquitoes for pesticide resistance.

Legislation

No explicit authority for federal assistance to states and localities for mosquito control existed when West Nile virus emerged in New York in 1999. CDC provided assistance to affected states pursuant to general disease control authorities of the Secretary of Health and Human Services in Title III of the Public Health Service Act, or authority provided in appropriations acts.

In 2003 Congress passed the Mosquito Abatement for Safety and Health Act (the MASH Act, P.L. 108-75), which authorizes the CDC Director to make assistance grants to states, and directly to political subdivisions of states. However, the MASH Act has not been implemented, and its appropriations authority expired in FY2007. In the 114th Congress, the Strengthening Mosquito Abatement for Safety and Health (SMASH) Act (S. 3039/H.R. 5492) would, among other things, extend the MASH Act, authorizing the appropriation of $130 million for each of FY2016-FY2021. The bills have not advanced in the 114th Congress.

The Administration has requested FY2016 supplemental appropriations to address the Zika threat. The House has passed a conference agreement (H.R. 2577) to provide such funds, which include assistance for mosquito control. The Senate has voted twice not to invoke cloture on the measure. More information is available in CRS Report R44549, *Supplemental Appropriations for Zika Response: The FY2016 Conference Agreement in Brief.*

The conference agreement also contains a provision (Division C) that would temporarily exempt EPA-registered pesticides from permitting requirements under the Clean Water Act (CWA). At issue is the whether the regulatory burden that CWA permitting places upon mosquito control agencies is needed to ensure that waterbodies do not become impaired or threatened by pesticides. For more information, see CRS Report RL32884, *Pesticide Use and Water Quality: Are the Laws Complementary or in Conflict?*

Sarah A. Lister, slister@crs.loc.gov, 7-7320
Grant D. Clinkingbeard, gclinkingbeard@crs.loc.gov, 7-6228

IF10439

Zika Poses New Challenges for Blood Centers

August 4, 2016 (IN10544)

Related Authors

- C. Stephen Redhead

- Sarah A. Lister

C. Stephen Redhead, Specialist in Health Policy (credhead@crs.loc.gov, 7-2261)

Sarah A. Lister, Specialist in Public Health and Epidemiology (slister@crs.loc.gov, 7-7320)

Introduction

On July 27, the Food and Drug Administration (FDA) advised blood centers in Miami-Dade and Broward counties in Florida to stop collecting blood until they could test each donated unit for Zika virus (ZIKV). OneBlood, which operates blood centers throughout most of the state, had already decided, after consulting with the Florida Department of Health (FDOH), to suspend collections in south Florida.

Two days later, FDOH announced the first cases of local (i.e., mosquito-borne) ZIKV transmission in the continental United States, originating in Miami-Dade county. Also, OneBlood announced that it would immediately begin testing of all blood units collected throughout its service area using an investigational test that FDA cleared for use earlier this year.

These are the latest in a series of steps to prevent the spread of ZIKV in the blood supply. In February, FDA released a set of donor screening and deferral recommendations, which U.S. blood banks implemented. FDA also advised suspending blood collections in areas where ZIKV was being spread by mosquitoes until testing could be implemented.

The Zika-related donor deferrals have exacerbated an already tight U.S. blood supply this summer. Last month, the nation's blood bankers issued a jo nt appeal for blood donors to sustain inventories across the country.

Figure 1. An American Red Cross Worker Prepares Donated Blood for Testing

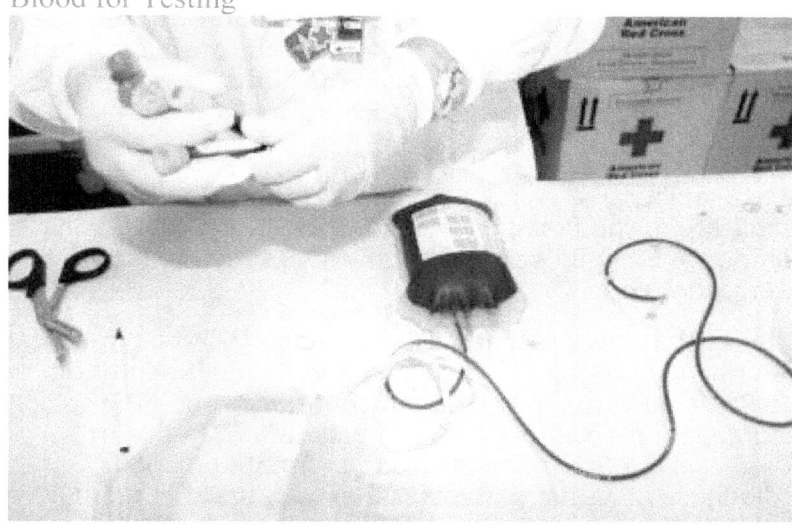

Source: U.S. Department of Defense, 2006.

Evolution of the Zika Threat

The Zika virus, first recognized in Uganda in 1947, is thought to have emerged in the Western Hemisphere early in 2015. Although most cases of ZIKV infection are mild, prenatal infection can cause severe birth defects, including microcephaly. ZIKV is transmitted among humans by the bite of an infected mosquito, by sexual contact, from mother to fetus, and through contaminated blood transfusion. ZIKV has spread from South America into Central America and the Caribbean. Puerto Rico has been hard hit, with more than 5,600 confirmed infections to date.

On July 29, FDOH reported four cases of mosquito-borne transmission of ZIKV originating from one neighborhood in Miami, the first such cases in the continental United States. An additional 11 cases from the same neighborhood were identified over the next few days. Six of these people had no symptoms of illness.

The Centers for Disease Control and Prevention (CDC) has issued public health guidance to stem further spread in this area, included an unprecedented recommendation that pregnant women avoid travel to the affected neighborhood. Local officials have expanded mosquito control efforts, but the effectiveness of these efforts is in question.

Response of FDA and the Blood Banks

On February 16, 2016, FDA issued donor education, screening, and deferral recommendations for immediate implementation to reduce the risk of transmitting ZIKV by blood transfusion. The agency had concluded that transfusion-transmitted ZIKV was likely, based on possible cases in Brazil and other evidence. Transmission of ZIKV by transfusion was subsequently confirmed.

FDA provided two sets of recommendations. One was for U.S. blood centers in *areas without local transmission*, which at the time included the entire continental United States. For those centers, FDA advised deferring—for four weeks—potential donors who (1) reported traveling to an area with active ZIKV transmission, (2) engaged in behaviors (including sexual contact) that may have exposed them to ZIKV, or (3) reported symptoms suggestive of ZIKV infection.

In *areas with local transmission*, which at the time included only Puerto Rico, FDA was more prescriptive. It recommended suspending blood collections until a ZIKV test was available and, in the meantime, procuring blood products from areas without local transmission. In early March, the Department of Health and Human Services announced that it would coordinate and pay for shipments of blood products to Puerto Rico from blood centers in the continental United States.

On March 30, FDA announced the availability of a test for ZIKV in donated blood under an Investigational New Drug (IND) application, the first of two such tests. Blood centers in Puerto Rico quickly resumed collections and began sending samples to a testing facility in Florida that had implemented the investigational ZIKV test.

OneBlood is one of several blood banks that have recently implemented ZIKV testing under the IND protocol. To date, it is the only one testing blood collected in the continental United States where local mosquito-borne ZIKV transmission has been confirmed. The other blood banks have implemented ZIKV testing as a precaution. FDA will use data from the IND protocols to evaluate the tests for licensure. (The IND test used for donated blood is different from ZIKV tests used to diagnose illness in patients. Currently, there are no FDA-approved ZIKV diagnostic tests, but FDA has granted emergency use authorizations—EUAs—for several tests under development.)

The affected Miami-Dade neighborhood may be the first of a number of "hot spots" of local ZIKV transmission expected this summer and fall on the U.S. mainland. This incident suggests that universal unit testing may be needed to adequately protect the blood supply in some areas before local transmission of ZIKV is detected.

However, during the summer, with donors on vacation and colleges out of session, blood centers often struggle to maintain adequate inventories. The ZIKV donor deferral is just one of several factors making the summer of 2016 even more challenging for blood centers than usual.

In May, blood centers raised the minimum hemoglobin level required for males to donate, one of a series of changes in a recent FDA rule that updated and revised existing blood banking regulations. An initial survey of blood banks indicated that this has caused a 2.4% loss of male donors. In June, FDA announced the recall of multiple lots of blood products with unacceptably high white blood cell counts due to a faulty filtering device. White blood cells typically are filtered out to reduce the risk of an adverse reaction caused by the transfusion recipient's own immune response to the foreign cells.

Stafford Act Assistance for Public Health Incidents

August 11, 2016 (IN10551)

Related Authors

Bruce R. Lindsay

Francis X. McCarthy

Bruce R. Lindsay, Analyst in American National Government (blindsay@crs.loc.gov, 7-3752)

Francis X. McCarthy, Analyst in Emergency Management Policy (fmccarthy@crs.loc.gov, 7-9533)

This Insight provides a brief overview of Stafford Act declarations under the Robert T. Stafford Disaster Relief and Emergency Assistance Act (hereinafter the Stafford Act—42 U.S.C. 5721 et seq.) and the types of assistance that could be authorized in response to public health incidents in general, and infectious disease incidents such as the Zika virus outbreak in particular. This Insight also provides examples of Stafford Act declarations that have been previously issued to address such incidents.

Overview

The Stafford Act authorizes the President to issue two types of declarations that could provide federal assistance to states and localities in response to a public health incident: a "major disaster declaration" or an "emergency declaration."

Major Disaster Declarations

Major disaster declarations authorize a wide range of federal assistance to states, local governments, tribal nations, individuals and households, and certain nonprofit organizations to recover from catastrophic incidents. Major disaster declarations must be requested by the state governor or tribal leader. The Stafford Act defines a major disaster as:

> any natural catastrophe (including any hurricane, tornado, storm, high water, wind-driven water, tidal wave, tsunami, earthquake, volcanic eruption, landslide, mudslide, snowstorm, or drought), or, regardless of cause, any fire, flood, or explosion, in any part of the United States, which in the determination of the President causes damage of sufficient severity and magnitude to warrant major disaster assistance under this chapter to supplement the efforts and available resources of states, local governments, and disaster relief organizations in alleviating the damage, loss, hardship, or suffering caused thereby (42 U.S.C. §5122(2)).

The list of events that qualify for a major disaster declaration is specific. There is no precedent for a major disaster declaration in response to a public health incident of any type, including infectious disease outbreaks, and it is unclear if such an incident would be eligible for a major disaster declaration.

Major Disaster Declaration Assistance

Assistance generally takes three forms: Public Assistance (PA), Individual Assistance (IA) and Hazard Mitigation Assistance (HMA). PA addresses essential needs of the state or tribe in response to an incident, including repairing damage to public infrastructure (public roads, buildings, etc.). IA helps families and individuals and can include temporary housing assistance and grants to address post-disaster needs (such as replacing clothing and furniture) as well as crisis counseling and disaster unemployment benefits. HMA provides the state with grant funding for state-identified mitigation projects.

Emergency Declarations

By comparison with a major disaster declaration, considerably less assistance is authorized under an emergency declaration. Emergency is defined more broadly than major disaster—which arguably may allow for greater eligibility of public health incidents. The Stafford Act defines an emergency as:

> any occasion or instance for which, in the determination of the President, federal assistance is needed to supplement State and local efforts and capabilities to save lives and to protect property and public health and safety, or to lessen or avert the threat of a catastrophe in any part of the United States (P.L. 93-288, 42 U.S.C. §5122(1)).

Emergency declarations can be issued before an incident when a threat is detected (for example, before a hurricane makes landfall or a river crests) to supplement and coordinate local and state response efforts. As traditionally implemented, the Stafford Act, however, does not supplant or supersede other federal authorities directed at public health incidents, such as those exercised by the Secretary of Health and Human Services.

Emergency Declaration Assistance

Emergency assistance can include two forms of PA; debris removal and emergency protective measures. Most assistance related to public health incidents has been delivered through emergency protective measures, which includes activities that are necessary to reduce an immediate threat to life, public health, or safety. Some forms of IA can be made available through an emergency declaration. Emergency declarations do not include HMA assistance.

Stafford Act Emergency Declarations for Public Health Incidents

Since the 1960s, the Stafford Act has been used sporadically for public health incidents. Some examples include the 1962 Louisiana and Mississippi chlorine barge accident and the evacuation of the New York Love Canal Chemical site in 1978. Below are examples of other emergency declarations for public health incidents since the 1990s.

West Nile Virus: New York and New Jersey

On October 11 and November 1, 2000, President Clinton issued emergency declarations for New York and New Jersey respectively to supplement state efforts to address the threat of the West Nile virus, a mosquito-borne virus. The assistance included state reimbursement of mosquito abatement eligible under the PA Program. These are the only instances of a Stafford Act declaration in response to an infectious disease incident.

West Virginia Chemical Spill

On January 10, 2014, President Obama issued an emergency declaration for the West Virginia chemical spill. The declaration helped deliver potable water and provided technical assistance to West Virginia State emergency management staff.

Flint, Michigan Water Contamination

On January 16, 2016, President Obama issued an emergency declaration for the State of Michigan for the Flint water contamination incident. The declaration provided water, water filters, water filter cartridges, water test kits, and other necessary related items.

For More Information

See CRS Report R43784, *FEMA's Disaster Declaration Process: A Primer*, *FEMA's Disaster Declaration Process: A Primer*; CRS Report R43990, *FEMA's Public Assistance Grant Program: Background and Considerations for Congress*; and CRS Report R42702, *Stafford Act Declarations 1953-2014: Trends, Analyses, and Implications for Congress*, for a complete background and details about Stafford Act Declarations.

This Insight provides a brief overview of Stafford Act declarations under the Robert T. Stafford Disaster Relief and Emergency Assistance Act (hereinafter the Stafford Act—42 U.S.C. 5721 et seq.) and the types of assistance that could be authorized in response to public health incidents in general, and infectious disease incidents such as the Zika virus outbreak in particular. This Insight also provides examples of Stafford Act declarations that have been previously issued to address such incidents.

Overview

The Stafford Act authorizes the President to issue two types of declarations that could provide federal assistance to states and localities in response to a public health incident: a "major disaster declaration" or an "emergency declaration."

Major Disaster Declarations

Major disaster declarations authorize a wide range of federal assistance to states, local governments, tribal nations, individuals and households, and certain nonprofit organizations to recover from catastrophic incidents. Major disaster declarations must be requested by the state governor or tribal leader. The Stafford Act defines a major disaster as:

> any natural catastrophe (including any hurricane, tornado, storm, high water, wind-driven water, tidal wave, tsunami, earthquake, volcanic eruption, landslide, mudslide, snowstorm, or drought), or, regardless of cause, any fire, flood, or explosion, in any part of the United States, which in the determination of the President causes damage of sufficient severity and

magnitude to warrant major disaster assistance under this chapter to supplement the efforts and available resources of states, local governments, and disaster relief organizations in alleviating the damage, loss, hardship, or suffering caused thereby (42 U.S.C. §5122(2)).

The list of events that qualify for a major disaster declaration is specific. There is no precedent for a major disaster declaration in response to a public health incident of any type, including infectious disease outbreaks, and it is unclear if such an incident would be eligible for a major disaster declaration.

Major Disaster Declaration Assistance

Assistance generally takes three forms: Public Assistance (PA), Individual Assistance (IA) and Hazard Mitigation Assistance (HMA). PA addresses essential needs of the state or tribe in response to an incident, including repairing damage to public infrastructure (public roads, buildings, etc.). IA helps families and individuals and can include temporary housing assistance and grants to address post-disaster needs (such as replacing clothing and furniture) as well as crisis counseling and disaster unemployment benefits. HMA provides the state with grant funding for state-identified mitigation projects.

Emergency Declarations

By comparison with a major disaster declaration, considerably less assistance is authorized under an emergency declaration. Emergency is defined more broadly than major disaster—which arguably may allow for greater eligibility of public health incidents. The Stafford Act defines an emergency as:

> any occasion or instance for which, in the determination of the President, federal assistance is needed to supplement State and local efforts and capabilities to save lives and to protect property and public health and safety, or to lessen or avert the threat of a catastrophe in any part of the United States (P.L. 93-288, 42 U.S.C. §5122(1)).

Emergency declarations can be issued before an incident when a threat is detected (for example, before a hurricane makes landfall or a river crests) to supplement and coordinate local and state response efforts. As traditionally implemented, the Stafford Act, however, does not supplant or supersede other federal authorities directed at public health incidents, such as those exercised by the Secretary of Health and Human Services.

Emergency Declaration Assistance

Emergency assistance can include two forms of PA; debris removal and emergency protective measures. Most assistance related to public health incidents has been delivered through emergency protective measures, which includes activities that are necessary to reduce an immediate threat to life, public health, or safety. Some forms of IA can be made available through an emergency declaration. Emergency declarations do not include HMA assistance.

Stafford Act Emergency Declarations for Public Health Incidents

Since the 1960s, the Stafford Act has been used sporadically for public health incidents. Some examples include the 1962 Louisiana and Mississippi chlorine barge accident and the evacuation of the New York Love Canal Chemical site in 1978. Below are examples of other emergency declarations for public health incidents since the 1990s.

West Nile Virus: New York and New Jersey

On October 11 and November 1, 2000, President Clinton issued emergency declarations for New York and New Jersey respectively to supplement state efforts to address the threat of the West Nile virus, a mosquito-borne virus. The assistance included state reimbursement of mosquito abatement eligible under the PA Program. These are the only instances of a Stafford Act declaration in response to an infectious disease incident.

West Virginia Chemical Spill

On January 10, 2014, President Obama issued an emergency declaration for the West Virginia chemical spill. The declaration helped deliver potable water and provided technical assistance to West Virginia State emergency management staff.

Flint, Michigan Water Contamination

On January 16, 2016, President Obama issued an emergency declaration for the State of Michigan for the Flint water contamination incident. The declaration provided water, water filters, water filter cartridges, water test kits, and other necessary related items.

For More Information

See CRS Report R43784, *FEMA's Disaster Declaration Process: A Primer*, *FEMA's Disaster Declaration Process: A Primer*; CRS Report R43990, *FEMA's Public Assistance Grant Program: Background and Considerations for Congress*; and CRS Report R42702, *Stafford Act Declarations 1953-2014: Trends, Analyses, and Implications for Congress*, for a complete background and details about Stafford Act Declarations.

The Zika Outbreak Is Declared a Public Health Emergency in Puerto Rico

August 17, 2016 (IN10555)

Related Author

Sarah A. Lister

Sarah A. Lister, Specialist in Public Health and Epidemiology (slister@crs.loc.gov, 7-7320)

On August 12, 2016, Sylvia Matthews Burwell, the Secretary of Health and Human Services (HHS), declared a public health emergency for Puerto Rico "[a]s a consequence of the outbreak of Zika virus and its potential effect on pregnant women and children born to pregnant women with Zika."

Background

The Zika virus (ZIKV), first recognized in Uganda in 1947, emerged in South America early in 2015. Although most cases of infection are mild, prenatal infection can cause severe birth defects, including microcephaly. ZIKV is transmitted among humans by the bite of an infected mosquito, by sexual contact, from mother to fetus, and through contaminated blood transfusions. Protecting pregnant women from infection is a public health priority.

ZIKV has spread from South America to Central America and the Caribbean. About 2,000 infections have been reported on the U.S. mainland, mostly among travelers from countries with widespread mosquito-borne ZIKV transmission. To date, only one neighborhood in Florida has experienced local (i.e., mosquito-borne) transmission.

In contrast, Puerto Rico has been hard hit. Local transmission on the island was first recognized in November 2015. Since then, more than 10,000 cases have been reported, more than 1,000 of them in pregnant women. Mosquito control measures have faltered, and

Dr. Thomas R. Frieden, Director of the U.S. Centers for Disease Control and Prevention (CDC), said that data from July showed an "explosion" of ZIKV cases.

In February 2016 the Administration requested supplemental funding of $1.9 billion for the Zika response, including primary care, maternal and child health, and Medicaid assistance for Puerto Rico. Congress has considered but not passed a supplemental appropriation to date, and HHS has reprogrammed $670 million in funds from other sources for its domestic and international response efforts.

Figure 1. Portion of a Brochure in Spanish Urging Protection from Mosquito Bites

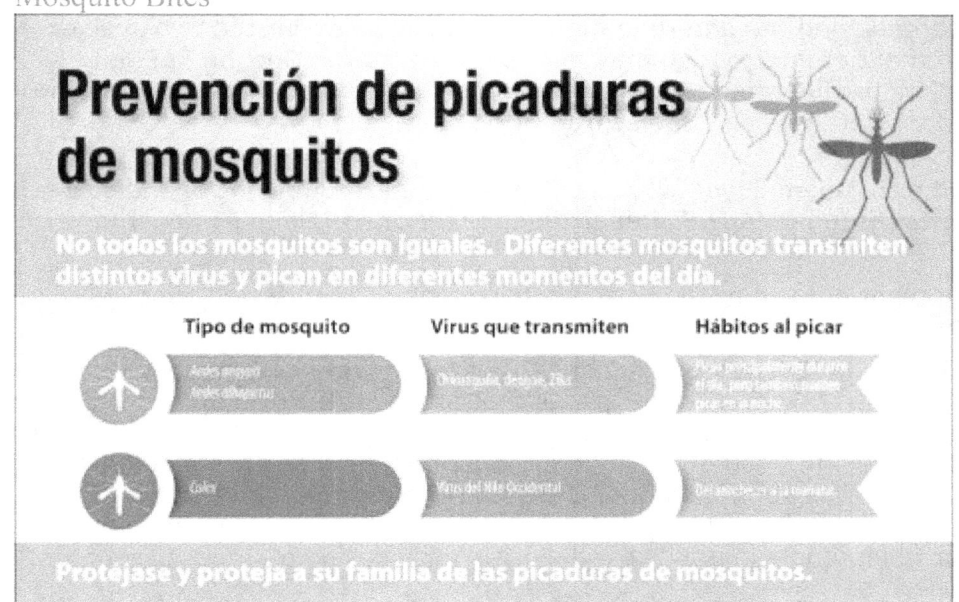

Source: Centers for Disease Control and Prevention (CDC) and the Departamento de Salud del Estado Libre Asociado de Puerto Rico (Puerto Rico Department of Health), "Información Sobre el Virus del Zika" (Information About the Zika Virus), http://www.salud.gov.pr/Sobre-tu-Salud/Pages/Condiciones/Zika.aspx.

Public Health Emergency Declaration Authority

The term "public health emergency" is used generically to refer to a variety of situations that involve threats to life and health, or threats to health system infrastructure. Federal and state laws use the term in various contexts to trigger broad or specific response authorities or to release additional funds.

On August 12, HHS Secretary Burwell declared the Zika outbreak to be a public health emergency pursuant to Section 319 of the Public Health Service Act (PHSA), 42 U.S.C. §247d, one of several public health emergency legal authorities available to her. The "Section 319" authority may be invoked if the Secretary "determines ... that—(1) a disease or disorder presents a public health emergency; or (2) a public health emergency, including significant outbreaks of infectious diseases or bioterrorist attacks, otherwise exists."

A determination under Section 319, alone or concurrent with other legal provisions, allows the Secretary to take certain actions not otherwise authorized, including (among others)

- awarding grants or contracts; and studying the causes, treatment, or prevention of the relevant disease or disorder;
- waiving certain management and reporting requirements of grantees; and
- streamlining federal hiring and payment procedures for response personnel.

Although a Section 319 determination also allows the Secretary to access a Public Health Emergency Fund for response purposes, there have not been any funds in this account since 2000.

The Declaration as Applied to the Zika Response in Puerto Rico

In a press release accompanying the determination, Secretary Burwell listed two specific actions that the government of Puerto Rico may take pursuant to the Section 319 determination. Each of them allows federal funds to support personnel in Puerto Rico who work on the ZIKV response effort. The enabled authorities are as follows:

- funding to hire and train unemployed workers to assist in mosquito control and outreach and education efforts through the U.S. Department of Labor's (DOL's) National Dislocated Worker Grant (DWG) program; and
- temporary reassignment of local public health department or agency personnel who are funded through PHSA programs in Puerto Rico to assist in the Zika response.

The DWG program, which is authorized by Section 170 of the Workforce Innovation and Opportunity Act (WIOA; P.L. 113-128), funds grants that are awarded primarily to states and local Workforce Development Boards (WDBs) to provide services for eligible individuals. Eligible workers include those dislocated by economic conditions, military installation closures, and emergency or disaster conditions. DWG services include job search assistance and training for eligible workers. In addition, DWG funding may be used to provide direct employment ("disaster relief employment") to individuals for a period of up to 12 months for work related to a disaster.

Typically DOL's authority to award disaster relief grants under the DWG program would be triggered by a declaration under the Robert T. Stafford Disaster Relief and Emergency Assistance Act (the Stafford Act). However, because the ZIKV outbreak has not led to a Stafford Act declaration to date, the Section 319 determination enables the DWGs pursuant to WIOA Section 170(a)(1)(B) (29 U.S.C. §3225(a)(1)(B)), regarding "an emergency or disaster situation of national significance that could result in a potentially large loss of employment, as declared or otherwise recognized by the chief official of a Federal agency with authority for or jurisdiction over the Federal response to the emergency or disaster situation."

In addition, PHSA Section 319(e) authorizes the HHS Secretary, upon gubernatorial request, to allow state, local, or tribal government employees who are supported by federal grants under any PHSA authority to work temporarily on the public health emergency response instead, without loss of funding. The PHSA provides authority, at least in part, for eight agencies and several offices in HHS, and their grant-making activities. The Section 319 declaration for Puerto Rico does not clarify which PHSA grants may be affected in this case.

Genetically Engineered Mosquitoes: A Vector Control Technology for Reducing Zika Virus Transmission

Background

In February 2016, the World Health Organization (WHO) declared Zika virus a "public health emergency of international concern." WHO defines such a public health emergency (1) to constitute a public health risk to other states through the international spread of disease, and (2) to potentially require a coordinated international response. This definition implies a situation that is serious, unusual, or unexpected; carries implications for public health beyond the affected state's national border; and may require immediate international action. (See CRS Insight IN10433, *Zika Virus: Global Health Considerations*.)

While only about one out of five persons infected with Zika virus exhibit even the common symptoms of mild fever, rash, and joint pain, the U.S. Centers for Disease Control and Prevention (CDC) have confirmed that Zika-infected pregnant women are at risk for delivering babies with microcephaly, a birth defect of the cerebral cortex where a baby's head is smaller than expected when compared to babies of the same sex and age. While research is limited, pregnant women are considered at risk for delivering babies with microcephaly no matter the stage of their pregnancy when they become infected with Zika virus. (See CRS Report R44368, *Zika Virus: Basics About the Disease*.)

Zika virus has now triggered outbreaks in 33 countries and territories, although confirmed cases linking Zika virus to babies with birth defects have thus far been seen in only Brazil and French Polynesia. Several countries have also reported a spike in cases of Guillain-Barré syndrome, a neurological syndrome, also believed to be an effect of the virus in some victims.

A Mosquito-Borne Virus

Zika virus (so named for the Zika forest in Uganda, where it was first identified in monkeys in 1947) is a mosquito-borne *flavivirus* that has rapidly infected human populations in Latin America and the Caribbean, including outbreaks in the U.S. territories of Puerto Rico, the U.S. Virgin Islands, and American Samoa. As of April 2016, over 400 cases in the United States have been confirmed, each acquired through either travel to areas where the mosquito vectors for Zika virus circulate or sexual contact with people who had traveled to such areas. No confirmed cases of local transmission have been confirmed in the contiguous United States as yet.

The first outbreak of Zika virus outside Africa, Asia, and the Pacific Islands occurred in Brazil in May 2015. The virus is spread predominantly by the female *Aedes aegypti* mosquito (and to a less effective extent by *Aedes albopictus*), an aggressive day-biter that is also a vector for yellow fever, dengue, and chikungunya. *Aedes aegypti* mosquitoes are non-native to the United States. A model created by Toronto researchers found that approximately 63% of the U.S. population lives in areas where Zika virus might spread during seasonally warm months if mosquitoes in the United States were to become vectors of Zika virus. As much as 7% of Americans live in areas where the cold might not kill off the mosquito in the winter, leaving them vulnerable year round. (See CRS InFocus 10353, *Mosquitoes, Zika Virus, and Transmission Ecology*.)

No vaccine exists for Zika, and scientists have estimated that it could take two years or more to develop such a remedy. Mosquito control and bite prevention are the first lines of defense. Controlling *Aedes aegypti* by conventional methods such as truck and aerial spraying is only moderately effective in reducing mosquito populations—approximately 30%-50%—in part owing to the resistance the mosquitoes have developed to the more commonly used insecticides and to the limited area in which *Aedes aegypti* mosquitoes circulate (100-200 yards from where the larvae emerge). *Aedes aegypti* mosquitoes also tend to favor house interiors where spraying/fogging is not practical. Strategic placement of several low-cost autocidal gravid ovitraps (which mimic breeding sites) in house interiors can reduce the *Aedes aegypti* population by about 50%.

Further contributing to the urgency of the pandemic, the El Niño weather phenomenon in 2015-2016 brought warmer temperatures and moisture to the regions most affected by Zika virus, and with that weather pattern, a potential increase in the population of *Aedes aegypti* mosquitoes.

OX513A Genetically Engineered Mosquitoes

In this environment, the creation of a genetically engineered (GE) *Aedes aegypti* mosquito by the British firm Oxitec in 2002, known as OX513A, is generating significant interest among public health officials. Developed originally to suppress the incidence of dengue fever, OX513A is now regarded as a promising technology to reduce the incidence of Zika virus transmission by reducing the population of mosquitoes. Oxitec is owned by Maryland-based Intrexon Corporation.

Oxitec's OX513A are mosquitoes that have been genetically engineered with a dominant transgene that produces a lethal protein that ties up the transcriptional machinery in the cells. The gene is passed on to the mosquito's offspring so that they die before reaching adulthood. Each OX513A mosquito is also engineered with a fluorescent marker that permits effective monitoring of larvae to assess the effectiveness of control. The fluorescent marker is visible using a specialist microscope in all

OX5213A offspring. The OX513A male mosquitoes, which do not bit or spread the virus are reared in laboratories and then released to mate with wild *Aedes aegypti* female mosquitoes.

Since only the females bite, releasing millions of OX513A males to mate with wild females, who would then produce larvae that die, could reduce the population of *Aedes aegypti* mosquitoes and, thereby, reduce the risk of Zika virus transmission to humans. This approach targets only the *Aedes aegypti* mosquitoes that can spread disease, because the OX513A males produce offspring only with their own species.

OX513A mosquitoes can be bred for generations and multiplied. Adult males with Oxitec's lethal transgene survive in the environment for only about a week. The OX513A mosquitoes also have the advantage of repressing populations of *Aedes aegypti* mosquitoes that carry insecticide resistance genes. According to peer-reviewed studies, of the more than 150 million OX513A mosquitoes released to date in field trials, no effects on other species have been observed, no evolution of resistance to the lethal transgene has been seen, and there has been no mating with non-target mosquitoes detected.

According to peer-reviewed studies, releases of OX513A males in the Cayman Islands in 2010 led to 90% suppression of the wild *Aedes aegypti* population. Isolated field demonstrations in Brazil have also achieved similarly successful results after six to nine months. In 2011, Oxitec conducted a sustained series of OX513A field releases in Itaberaba, a suburb of Juazeiro in the semi-arid northeast region of Brazil. Normal mosquito control continued during the field study as public health agents continued to destroy breeding sites and treat homes with larvicide. According to peer-reviewed studies, the *Aedes aegypti* population was reduced by over 90% in a year based on data from multiple locations.

Brazil's National Biosafety Commission approved country-wide use of OX513A in 2014, making Brazil the first country to approve the commercial use of the OX513A mosquitoes. A year later, the OX513A mosquitoes were released in the Brazilian city of Piracicaba and, in January 2016, announced plans to scale up the program and expand their OX513A production capacity. Panama also field tested the OX513A mosquitoes in 2014.

In April 2016, Brazil's National Health Surveillance Agency announced that it would grant Oxitec a temporary registration to deploy the genetically engineered mosquitoes throughout the country. The agency is now developing new rules to provide Brazil with a regulatory framework to address the OX513A mosquitoes, as well as other genetically engineered insects that may be developed in the future. WHO has issued a positive recommendation in support of the OX513A mosquitoes. In addition, the Pan-American Health Organization has also announced that it will provide technical support for countries that wish to implement the OX513A mosquitoes.

Some researchers have raised questions about the OX513A mosquitoes' fitness for breeding, and whether the males could evolve resistance to the lethal gene. Males are mechanically sorted in the laboratory, resulting in less than 0.01% females accidently released. This could lead to a small but temporary increase in the number of biting mosquitoes. A possible solution currently being explored by Oxitec and the University of California-Irvine is a genetic modification to make females unable to fly. If successful, this approach would make these 0.01% released females unable to mate or bite.

U.S. Environmental Assessment of GE Mosquitoes

Oxitec applied for a permit to field test the OX513A mosquitoes in the Florida Keys in 2011. On April 3, 2012, the Key West City Commission passed a resolution objecting to the release of the OX513A mosquitoes. The U.S. Food and Drug Administration Center for Veterinary Medicine (FDA-CVM) led an examination of OX513A under its Investigational New Animal Drug regulatory process. FDA's review team was comprised of experts from the CVM, the CDC, and the U.S. Environmental Protection Agency. On March 11, 2016, FDA published its Preliminary Finding of No Significant Impact (FONSI) for proposed field testing the OX513A mosquito in the Florida Keys. After a 60-day comment period, FDA published its final EA and associated FONSI on August 5, 2016, which allows Oxitec to begin field trials.

This review team examined Oxitec's and independent collaborators published evidence from their Brazil and Cayman Islands field trials and other data on safety studies. FDA found that the probability that the release of OX513A male mosquitoes would result in toxic or allergenic effects in humans or other animals is negligible. "Almost all of the OX513A mosquitoes released for the investigational field trial will be male, and male mosquitoes do not bite humans or other animals. They are therefore not expected to have any direct impacts on human or animal health." FDA also found that the "probability that the release or rearing of OX513A mosquitoes would have adverse impacts on the ecosystem is largely negligible" and that the "probability of OX513A mosquitoes and their progeny persisting and establishing at the proposed trial site or spreading beyond its boundaries is extremely unlikely."

With the FONSI, Oxitec plans to begin field testing in Key Haven, Florida, in collaboration with the Florida Keys Mosquito Control District. However, the Florida Keys Environmental Coalition and others have petitioned the Florida Commissioner of Agriculture and Consumer Services to halt any field testing of the OX513A mosquitoes in the state. As of August 2016, the Florida Keys Mosquito Control Board has not approved the trial release, instead putting it on the November ballot as a non-binding referendum. Oxitec has asked FDA to consider releasing the mosquitoes on an emergency basis elsewhere.

Congress has oversight of FDA regulations and appropriations. Annual appropriations for the CDC are also under congressional authority. If the United States supports stepped-up international efforts to reduce the incidence of Zika transmission, appropriations to the United States Agency for International Development could play an important role.

Tadlock Cowan, tcowan@crs.loc.gov, 7-7600

IF10401

www.ingramcontent.com/pod-product-compliance
Lightning Source LLC
Chambersburg PA
CBHW081327310526

45789CB00018B/2467